Maritime Operational Law

Maritime Operational Law

U C Jha
Kishore Kumar Khera

Vij Books
New Delhi (India)

First Published in India in 2023

Published by

Vij Books
(An imprint of Vij Books India Pvt Ltd)

(Publishers, Distributors & Importers)
4836/24, Ansari Road
Delhi - 110 002
Phones: 91-11-43596460, Mob: 98110 94883
e-mail: contact@vijpublishing.com
web : www.vijbooks.in

ISBN: 978-81-19438-83-9 (PB)

Contents

In the Harbour

India has a unique maritime geography with a central location and reach across the Indian Ocean Region (IOR). The Indian Ocean basin is particularly important for India as the region's most populous country and geopolitical keystone. India's 90 percent of trade by volume and almost all oil imports come via sea route, underscoring the region's significance. The strategic importance of IOR is ever-increasing to the world order in general and the Indian sub-continent in particular.

The primary objective of the Indian Navy is to safeguard the nation's maritime borders, and in conjunction with other armed forces of the union, act to deter or defeat any threats or aggression against the territory, people or maritime interests of India, both in war and peace. The full range of operations in which the Indian maritime forces may be involved is vast, ranging from high-intensity warfighting at one end to humanitarian assistance and disaster relief operations at the other. This broad continuum of operational roles can be broken down into distinct roles, each demanding a specific set of legal regimes.

The "operational law" is a relatively new term that has come into use in the last two decades to describe various bodies of national and international laws which apply to and regulate the planning and conduct of military operations. These include customary international law, such as the law governing the use of force (*jus ad bellum*), the law of armed conflict (LOAC) or international humanitarian law (IHL), international human rights law, the law of the sea, and military use of air space; as well as various types of national laws such as military criminal justice and disciplinary regulations, as contained in the Indian Navy Act, 1957, and the Naval Regulations.

The Indian Maritime Doctrine (2015) refers to the Great Epic *Mahabharata* (3139 BC), and Kautilya's *Arthashastra* (322-298 BC), which govern justification for war (*Jus ad Bellum*) and the conduct in war (*Jus in Bello*). In the time of the *Mahabharata*, warfare was restricted to between sunrise and sunset, to be fought between equals, on a designated battlefield, with attack prohibited against defenceless or wounded persons. Kautilya's *Arthashastra* conceptualised the justification for war and described in detail the various conditions and rationale for going to war and the means and methods of fighting a war.[1]

The concept *jus ad bellum* constitutes an important component of the international law of military operations; it is closely linked to the other bodies of law that may come into play. It relates to the justification for resorting to armed force. The principal justification is the right to individual or collective self-defence, which is an inherent right as laid down in Article 51 of the UN Charter,[2] and the Constitution of India. These legitimise the use of force to defend one's territory, forces and nationals in various conditions, such as response to an armed attack. The first task of a judge advocate during a military operation is defining what legal authority justifies the operation itself.[3]

The conduct of hostilities or *jus in bello* is the most significant legal regime impacting military operations. Today, *jus in bello* is divided into two

---

1 Indian Maritime Doctrine 2009, Indian Navy, Naval Strategic Publication 1.1, updated online version 2015, Integrated Headquarters, Ministry of Defence (Navy) 2015, pp. 174, at p. 30. Also see: Ensuring Secure Seas: Indian Maritime Security Strategy, Integrated Headquarters, Ministry of Defence (Navy), 2015, p. 185.

2 The UN Charter essentially outlaws the use of force, authorizing it only pursuant to a Security Council resolution issued under Chapter VII, while preserving and recognizing in Article 51 the inherent right to self-defence, including collective self-defence. Prior to the establishment of the UN Charter, international law recognized a variety of legal bases permitting a nation's resort to the use of force against another nation. In fact, some form of *jus ad bellum* has existed for as long as war, although it was largely municipal in nature; applicable only to the specific civilizations that adopted them. Gill Terry D. and Fleck Dieter, 2015, *The Handbook of the International Law of Military Operations*, Oxford: Oxford University Press, pp. 657, at p. 16.

3 Fixdal and Smith (1998) have elaborated 'just war criteria by category': *Jus ad bellum*: (1) Right authority: Only a legitimate authority has the right to declare a war. (2) Just cause: We are not only permitted but may be required to use lethal force if we have a just cause. (3) Right intention: In war, not only the cause and the goals must be just, but also our motive for responding to the cause and taking up the goals. (4) Last resort: We may resort to war only if it is the last viable alternative. (5) Proportionality: We must be confident that resorting to war will do more good than harm. (6) Reasonable hope: We must have reasonable grounds for believing the cause can be achieved. (7) Relative justice: No state can act if it proposes absolute justice. (8) Open declaration: An explicit formal statement is required before resorting to force. *Jus in bello*: (1) Discrimination: Non-combatants must be given immunity and protection. (2) Proportionality: Military actions must do more good than harm. Fixdal Mona and Smith Dan, Humanitarian Intervention and Just War, *Mershon International Studies Review*, Vol. 42, No. 2, November 1998, pp. 283–312.

major categories of conventions: the 'Laws of The Hague', and the 'Laws of Geneva'. The Law of The Hague is primarily concerned with regulating the means and methods of warfare. The Law of Geneva was developed in response to the terrible suffering wrought upon civilians and other victims of war. It is now contained in the Geneva Conventions of 1949, and their subsequent Protocols of 1977. In addition to this, there are a large number of treaties of recent origin which ban or regulate various kinds of weapons in an armed conflict.

The ongoing Russia-Ukraine military operation or one fought in Syria or others under the authority of international organisations such as the UN, NATO, or the African Union, are increasingly complex in character and involve a large number of states and other international actors, bringing the participating states and their armed forces into contact with a variety of different areas of international legal regulation. The international law of military operations is a mixed body of law. It is largely governed by customs, treaties, and the other sources governing various other disciplines of international law such as those relating to the use of force, international humanitarian law, international human rights law, or the law of the sea and air law. This manual has been prepared for the naval force in India as would apply to the Indian Naval Forces in their operations. All legal provisions discussed in this manual contain full references in the footnotes indicating the sources of legal obligation and their interpretation in academic or official publications. This Manual would also be of interest to the Indian Coast Guards,[4] as their ships and aircraft undertake regular patrols to enforce maritime laws, and other regulations and international treaties to which India is a signatory.

In comparison with armed conflicts on land, the past two decades have not seen many armed conflicts take place at sea (or in other waters). In the event of an armed conflict that takes place wholly or in part at sea, the provisions of the Geneva Convention II must already be known and their contemporary meaning understood. This understanding must be ensured in peacetime, including through prevention activities such as the training of armed forces and especially naval forces.

4 The Indian Coast Guard (ICG) came into being on 01 February 1977. The ICG is a maritime armed force operating under the Ministry of Defence. The duties and functions of the service were formally defined in the Coast Guard Act, which was passed by the Parliament on August 18, 1978. Geographically, the ICG functions through four Regional Headquarters located at Mumbai, Gandhi Nagar, Chennai and Port Blair.

This Manual of Maritime Operational Law attempts to provide as comprehensive an overview as possible of all areas of law relevant to maritime operations, including anti-piracy operations. While it is impossible to cover every single aspect of international law, the endeavour has been to provide a comprehensive scope and coverage of all the relevant issues. The Manual reflects the personal views of the authors. It restates the law of maritime operations to guide maritime commanders, officers, judge advocates, government officials and researchers.

New Delhi
15 September 2023

U C Jha
Kishore Kumar Khera

Section 1

Overview of Maritime Operational Law

I

Casting Off

Introduction

The sea has always been the major highway for international commerce. In the contemporary globalised economy, the relevance of sea transport in international trade is bigger than ever. Around 90 per cent of world trade depends on maritime transport; it is impossible to imagine a modern world without seafaring conveyance. Maritime transport remains the backbone of global trade and the global economy. It ensures that humanity remains connected through exports and imports. A strong navy is an important element of every maritime nation. It plays a significant role in safeguarding territory and trade, offensive operations against enemy forces, and defensive operations to protect its resources. There are many military missions in this role like Sea Control, Sea Denial, Blockade, Anti-piracy, Power Projection, etc, which have indirect fall-out for the protection of the maritime trade. The full range of operations in which a nation's naval forces may be involved is vast, ranging from high-intensity warfighting at one end to humanitarian assistance and disaster relief operations at the other. Today, modern navies are engaged in four kinds of operations: diplomatic, military, benign, and constabulary.[1]

1 The four main roles envisaged for the Indian Navy are: the military role, the diplomatic role, constabulary role, and benign role. The *raison d'etre* of the Navy is to ensure that no hostile maritime power degrades own national security and interests. The navy's military role is characterised by threat or use of force at and / or from the sea. This includes application of maritime power in both - offensive operations against enemy forces, territory and trade, and defensive operations to protect own forces, territory and trade. The larger purpose of navy's diplomatic role is to favourably shape the maritime environment in furtherance of national interests, in consonance with the nation's foreign policy and national security objectives. In the constabulary role, forces are employed to enforce law of the land or to implement a regime established by an international mandate. On the high seas, navies exercised exclusive flag State

Naval warfare is almost as old as conflicts between armies on land. While most nations have a long history of fighting on land, the list of countries having fought a naval war is relatively shorter. There have been few naval conflicts since 1945, and those that have occurred have been limited in scale. No such naval conflict has taken place between major maritime powers. However, navies have tripled in number since then, and today there are growing tensions between significant naval powers.[2]

Naval forces continue to be part of military operations. During the Falklands War in 1982, the British lost six ships. Other naval force operations include Afghanistan (2001), the Second Gulf War (2003), Lebanon (2006), Gaza (2009), Libya (2011), Ukraine (2014) and Syria (2015). While the conflict in Ukraine has been chiefly fought on land and in the skies, a few hostilities also played out in the naval domain. On April 14, 2022, the Russian warship Moskva, the largest Russian warship sunk in combat since World War II. Ukrainian officials claimed that their forces damaged the ship with two R-360 Neptune anti-ship missiles, a claim refuted by the Russian government.[3]

---

jurisdiction over their own States' merchant ships and other civilian vessels. They also engaged in antipiracy operations, ensuring that the seas were free for safe and secure trading activities. Force is only employed for self-defence or as a last resort in execution of this role. Benign tasks include humanitarian aid, disaster relief, Search and Rescue (SAR), ordnance disposal, diving assistance, salvage operations, hydrographic surveys, etc. Role of the Indian Navy, available at: https://indiannavy.nic.in/content/role-navy.

2 The growing appropriation of the oceans by states challenging the rules of international maritime law undermines the notion of the sea as an open space for movement and trade. Appropriation can be motivated by a desire to exploit the seas for natural resources, such as illegal gas drilling in the Mediterranean, or to restrict access to parts of the sea for reasons of territorial interest, such as in the China Sea. Appropriation runs the risk of generating territorial disputes backed by the implicit or explicit threat of the use of force (South China Sea, Eastern Mediterranean, or Arctic Ocean). Many states are committed to maintaining open and safe access to the high seas based on the principle of freedom of navigation and overflights. They deploy forces to ensure respect for international law and to protect their sovereignty and long-term interests. The EU: From Maritime Actor to Sea Power, Council of the European Union, Analysis and Research Tea, February 16, 2023, p. 16.

3 Traditionally, the public consciousness imagines naval warfare mainly as "warship-to-warship" engagements, contemporary history and current naval operations predominantly are different. Rather than conflict at sea, naval warfare increasingly involves contributing to armed conflict from the sea, in support of land operations. Illustratively, the Syrian conflict saw Russian warships firing missiles from the Caspian Sea onto Syrian territory, American warships engaged Syrian airfields from the Mediterranean Sea and the UK, during the North Atlantic Treaty Organization's (NATO's) Operation Unified Protector, struck targets in Libya from the sea. Fink

The law of naval warfare as it existed in 1899 and, as is understood 125 years later, exhibits a few similarities but many differences. The fundamental similarity is that the law of naval warfare consists primarily of customary international law. The many differences in this law have been caused by the major changes in the law of the sea. Today, war at sea involves nuclear-powered aircraft carriers; supersonic aircraft, helicopters and tilt-rotor aircraft; submarines; high-speed patrol craft; ballistic, cruise, and other guided missiles; long-range secure communications for command, control, computers, intelligence, surveillance, and reconnaissance; radar; underwater sound technology; electronic and information warfare; satellites in space; unmanned aerial and undersea vehicles; and stealth and computer technology; as well as expeditionary and amphibious capabilities. Nevertheless, the fundamental role of navies continues to be establishing control at sea or denying it to the enemy, linking that control to broad political and economic issues ashore.

The law of armed conflict (LOAC) or international humanitarian law (IHL) applicable at sea has not attracted much attention in the last few decades. The few instances of armed conflict at sea, have not brought seriously into question the detailed rules regulating it. There have been no naval cases dealt with by the international tribunals as compared with the law regulating armed conflict on land or in the air.[4]

Laws Relating to Naval Warfare

The laws regulating the conduct of war at sea were customary.[5] Early maritime law was designed to ameliorate conflict at sea. Perhaps the first law directly affecting sea power was the set of customary rules governing the law of "prize", i.e., the capture of vessels in wartime. In 1618, the Dutch jurist, Hugo Grotius, set forth the natural-law doctrine of "freedom of the seas", a concept that preserved access to the seas for all nations and thereby fuelled an explosion in international trade. By 1758, the Swiss lawyer Vattel

Martin, The ever-existing "crisis" of the law of naval warfare, *International Review of the Red Cross*, Vo. 104, No. 920-921,2022, pp. 1971-1988; Peter Beaumont, The sinking of the Moskva: what do we know, and why does it matter? *The Guardian*, April 15, 2022.

4 Hains Steven, War at sea: Nineteenth-century laws for twenty-first century wars? *International Review of the Red Cross*, Vol. 98 (2), 2016, pp. 419–447.

5 For initial development of the law relating to naval warfare see: Pomeroy John Norton, The Law of Maritime Warfare, as It Affects the Belligerents, *The North American Review*, Vol. 114, No. 235, April 1872, pp. 376- 407.

had expounded two fundamental principles of the law of neutrality that had gained widespread acceptance: belligerents were obligated to respect the neutrality of States remaining neutral, and a neutral State had a duty to remain impartial.

The development of the treaty law relating to naval warfare began with the Paris Declaration of 1856. The Paris Declaration established international policies related to neutral and belligerent shipping on the high seas, introducing new rules for prizes of war, a piece of enemy property seized by a belligerent party during or after a war or battle, typically at sea. The Declaration added the principle that blockades, to be binding, must be effective.[6] The first Hague Peace Conference, which met in 1899, adopted the Convention for the Adaptation to Maritime Warfare of the Principles of the Geneva Convention of 1864 (Hague III). The 1868 Additional Articles Relating to the Condition of Wounded in War provided protections for certain categories of persons at sea.

During the period between the Hague Peace Conferences of 1899 and 1907, the major international event in the military area was the Russo-Japanese War (1904-1905). The Russian agenda for the 1907 Second Hague Peace Conference called for the framing of a convention relative to the laws and customs of maritime warfare. There were eight naval conventions agreed upon in 1907, although only following five of them entered into force.[7]

- Hague Convention (VII) relating to the Conversion of Merchant Ships into War-Ships

6 The Treaty of Paris was signed March 30, 1856 which ended the Crimean War (1853-1856). The treaty was signed between Russia on one side and France, Great Britain, Sardinia-Piedmont, and Turkey on the other. Both sides recognized that they would not seize enemy goods on neutral vessels nor neutral goods on enemy vessels. The belligerents further proclaimed that they would not issue letters of marque. Virtually all states acceded to the Declaration. The United States, which aimed at a complete exemption of private property from capture at sea, withheld its formal adherence, its amendment not having been accepted by all the Powers. In 1861, at the beginning of the Civil War, the United States announced nevertheless that it would respect the principles of the Declaration for the duration of the hostilities. Declaration Respecting Maritime Law. Paris, 16 April 1856, Geneva: ICRC database.

7 These Conventions entered into force on January 26, 1910. The three Convention which did not enter into fore were: Hague Convention (VI) relative to the Legal Status of Enemy Merchant Ships at the Outbreak of Hostilities; Hague Convention X is now covered by the 1949 Geneva Convention II; and Hague Convention (XII) relative to the Establishment of an International Prize Court. The Prize Court law never entered into force because it did not secure any state ratification.

- Hague Convention (VIII) relative to the Laying of Automatic Submarine Contact Mines
- Hague Convention (IX) Concerning Bombardment by Naval Forces in Time of War
- Hague Convention (XI) relative to Certain Restrictions with regard to the Exercise of Capture in Naval War
- Hague Convention (XIII) Concerning the Rights and Duties of Neutral Powers in Naval War

This corpus of Hague law was complemented by the Helsinki Principles on the Law of Maritime Neutrality, which codified the rules applicable to the relations between parties to a conflict and provided that neutral States should be governed by the law of peace, not war. In 1909, however, the Declaration of London Concerning the Laws of Naval War adopted the doctrine of ultimate destination, which permitted the capture of absolute contraband, whether its route to an ultimate destination in enemy territory was direct or indirect and circuitous, through neutral state waters or ports. It was observed by several nations during World War I, although the document never entered into legal force.

Customary international law and the 1936 London Protocol prohibited the destruction of enemy merchant vessels unless the passengers and crew were first disembarked and their safety assured. This rule did not apply if the merchant's vessel resisted the belligerent's right to visit and search to determine the enemy character of the vessel. During World War II, however, both the Axis and the Allies disregarded this rule and intentionally targeted the merchant ships of the enemy.

Modern Laws

The modern law regulating naval and submarine operations could be constructed from three branches of international law: the law of the sea, the law of neutrality and the law of armed conflict (LOAC), also called international humanitarian law (IHL). The naval forces will be bound by only those IHL treaties which have been ratified by the State.

Geneva Conventions II of 1949

The Geneva Convention of 1864 embodied the principle that members of the armed forces who are *hors de combat* must be protected and cared for regardless of their nationality. However, the states were not ready to accept ICRC's proposal to extend this principle to armed forces at sea. The turning point was the 1866 Battle of Lissa in the Adriatic Sea. It caused a large number of deaths due to the lack of care and protection for the sick, wounded and shipwrecked. During the battle, a conference in 1868 adopted fifteen "Additional Articles relating to the Conditions of the Wounded in War". These articles addressed issues such as the protection of boats that collect the shipwrecked and wounded, hospital ships and the status of medical personnel. However, the reticence of the major naval powers prevented these articles from entering into force. In line with the ICRC's repeated calls to adapt the 1864 Geneva Convention to the conditions of warfare at sea, the First Hague Peace Conference of 1899 adopted Hague Convention III, drawing inspiration from the Additional Articles of 1868. Hague Convention III, which entered into force in 1900, was the first treaty to protect victims of armed conflict at sea. It was revised in 1907 in light of the new Geneva Convention of 1906 governing land warfare, resulting in the 1907 Hague Convention X on maritime warfare. This convention remained the governing treaty for the protection of members of armed forces at sea until the adoption of the Second Geneva Convention in 1949.[8]

The 1949 Geneva Conventions constitute the foundation of international humanitarian law today. They have been universally ratified or adhered to. The Geneva Convention contain the essential rules of humanitarian law protecting civilians, persons who are *hors de combat* and medical and religious personnel, as well as a range of protected objects such as civilian objects and medical units and transports. The Second Geneva Convention of 1949 has restated customary rules of IHL applicable to international armed conflict at sea. It does not govern the use of submarine warfare. The overall object and purpose of the Geneva Convention II[9] is to ensure respect for and protection of the wounded, sick and shipwrecked, as well as the dead, in international armed conflict at sea or other waters.

Article 1 of the Convention states that the High Contracting Parties undertake to respect and ensure respect for the present Convention in all

8 Demeyere Bruno, Jean-Marie Henckaerts, Heleen Hiemstra and Ellen Nohle, The updated ICRC Commentary on the Second Geneva Convention: Demystifying the law of armed conflict at sea, *International Review of the Red Cross*, Vol. 98(2), 2016, pp. 410-417.

9 The Geneva Convention for the Amelioration of the Condition of Wounded, Sick and Shipwrecked Members of Armed Forces at Sea is the second of four Conventions adopted by the Diplomatic Conference of Geneva of 1949 (Geneva Convention II).

circumstances. The phrase 'to respect and to ensure respect' applies first and foremost to the High Contracting Parties themselves, their armed forces, other persons and groups acting on their behalf, and their populations as a whole. The obligation to respect and ensure respect for the Conventions is not limited to armed conflict but applies equally in peacetime.[10] The provisions of Geneva Convention II apply to all cases of (i) declared war or of any other armed conflict which may arise between two or more of the High Contracting Parties, even if the state of war is not recognised by one of them; and (ii) partial or total occupation of the territory of a High Contracting Party, even if the said occupation meets with no armed resistance.[11]

As regards the field of application, Article 4 states that in case of hostilities between land and naval forces of Parties to the conflict, the provisions of the Geneva Convention II shall apply only to forces on board ships. Forces put ashore shall become subject to the provisions of the Geneva Convention for the Amelioration of the Condition of the Wounded and Sick in Armed Forces in the Field (Convention I). Article 7 is a cornerstone of the regime established by the Geneva Conventions. It provides, "Wounded, sick and shipwrecked persons, as well as members of the medical personnel and chaplains, may in no circumstances renounce in part or entirety the rights secured to them by the present Convention, and by the special agreements referred to in the foregoing Article, if such there be." The purpose of Article 7 is to ensure that protected persons enjoy the protection of the Conventions until the last moment when international humanitarian law applies to them or their situation. It states that the rights of protected persons are inalienable. The other provisions in the Convention are geared towards this purpose, for example, the rules on the search for and collection of the shipwrecked, wounded and sick and of the dead.

---

10 Article 1 obliges each High Contracting Party and its organs to respect the Geneva Conventions, and to ensure respect for these Conventions by the population over which it exercises authority and any other persons or groups whose conduct is attributable to it. This scope is demonstrated by the ordinary meaning of the term, subsequent agreements, subsequent practice and other relevant rules of international law. As a matter of good faith performance of the Conventions, each High Contracting Party also has a duty not to encourage violations by others. Robson Verity, The Common Approach to Article 1: The Scope of Each State's Obligation to Ensure Respect for the Geneva Conventions, *Journal of Conflict and Security Law*, Volume 25, Issue 1, Spring 2020, pp. 101–115.

11 Article 2, Geneva Convention II of 1949.

Article 18 requires the parties, after each engagement and without delay,[12] to take all possible measures to search for and collect the wounded, sick, shipwrecked and dead at sea, without discriminating between their own and enemy personnel. The good faith interpretation and implementation of this provision is of critical importance in order to achieve the objectives of the Second Geneva Convention. The wounded, sick and shipwrecked, once collected, must receive "adequate care" as soon as possible. This includes providing the medical care and attention required by their condition, as well as other forms of non-medical care, such as the provision of food, drinking water, shelter, clothing, and sanitary and hygiene items. The parties are furthermore required to record information that can assist in the identification of the wounded, sick, shipwrecked and dead, and to forward this information to the power on which they depend. This is crucial so that families can be appraised of the fate of their loved ones. Specific obligations about the dead include respectful and honourable treatment, burial, and respect for their resting place.[13]

In addition, the rules that require respect for and protection of medical and religious personnel, transports, such as hospital ships and coastal rescue craft, and the distinctive emblems all serve the purpose of protecting and caring for the shipwrecked, wounded and sick. The Second Convention has one annex, providing a model identity card for medical and religious personnel attached to the armed forces at sea.

12 A vessel that has launched a weapon from a considerable distance against an enemy warship or aircraft might not be able to implement "without delay" any of the obligations contemplated on the basis of Article 18, since it is not physically present in the vicinity of the casualties. Still, that vessel remains under an obligation to consider what measures are possible in light of the circumstances. This includes considering whether it is possible to take measures such as disclosing the geographic location of the attacked vessel or aircraft with as much precision as possible, not only to its land-based authorities but also to enemy and neutral vessels or impartial humanitarian organizations capable of conducting search and rescue operations. In this regard, the availability of new technology such as satellites and unmanned aerial platforms can enable a more accurate assessment of the number and location of the shipwrecked, wounded, sick and dead without requiring physical proximity to the attacked vessel or aircraft. Dorman Knut, Liesbeth Lijnzaad, Marco Sassoli and Philip Spoerri (ed.), 2017, *Revised Commentary on the Second Geneva Convention*, Cambridge: Cambridge University Press, Para 1645 and 1646.

13 Article 4, Second Geneva Convention of 1949.

The UN Convention on the Laws of Sea

The 1982 UN Convention on the Laws of Sea (UNCLOS) is the modern source of the law of the sea. The outbreak of an armed conflict at sea does not necessarily terminate or suspend the applicability of UNCLOS. Instead, it is internationally accepted that by and large, most provisions of UNCLOS will remain in operation in times of armed conflict, both in the relationship between the Parties to the conflict and, in the case of an international armed conflict, the relationship between the Parties to the conflict and neutral Powers. Thus, for example, the term 'warship', which is used several times in the Second Convention, has nowadays to be interpreted based on the requirements reflected in Article 29 of UNCLOS. Lastly, even if a State were to withdraw from UNCLOS, or suspend its operation, it remains bound by those of its rules which reflect customary international law. Those rules are equally binding upon States which have not become party to UNCLOS. In turn, some of the rules of UNCLOS state that they are to be exercised 'subject to this Convention and to other rules of international law', which includes international humanitarian law, i.e., the rules of naval warfare. This may lead to a temporary suspension of the applicability of an individual rule of UNCLOS, but not of the Convention as a whole.[14]

The Right to Participate in Hostilities at Sea

The legal competency to participate in naval warfare is available only to certain persons and platforms. They comprise warships and other units of naval armed forces, military aircraft, and land and air armed forces. Vessels and persons who may not undertake acts of naval warfare include merchant ships, civilian ships and boats such as fishing boats, civil aircraft, government-owned or -operated ships or aircraft that are not warships or military aircraft, and prize crews of captured ships. However, this does not affect the right of a state to convert a merchant vessel to a warship in

14 In addition, some rules of UNCLOS explicitly allow for the suspension of certain rights for security considerations, a notion which encompasses armed conflict. By way of example, reference can be made to Article 25(3) of UNCLOS. Under certain conditions, this provision allows a coastal State, 'without discrimination in form or in fact among foreign ships', to 'suspend temporarily in specified areas of its territorial sea the innocent passage of foreign ships if such suspension is essential for the protection of its security'. An armed conflict may qualify as such a circumstance. Wolff Heintschel von Heinegg, Methods and Means of Naval Warfare in Non-International Armed Conflicts, *International Law Studies*, US Naval War College, Vol. 88, 2012, pp. 211–236.

accordance with Hague Convention VII, 1907.[15] Convention VII does not clarify two questions: (a) whether conversion of a merchant's vessel can take place anywhere as well as at any time; and (b) whether the same ship may be reconverted back into a merchant's vessel before the termination of the war.[16]

Protected Entities

Protected Persons

Protected persons under Article 13 of the Second Geneva Convention of 1949 are the wounded, sick and shipwrecked at sea belonging to the following categories:

1. Members of the armed forces of a Party to the conflict, as well as members of militias or volunteer corps forming part of such armed forces.

2. Members of other militias and members of other volunteer corps, etc.; who (a) are commanded by a person responsible for his subordinates; (b) have a fixed distinctive sign recognisable at a distance; (c) carry arms openly; and (d) conduct their operations in accordance with the laws and customs of war.

3. Members of regular armed forces who profess allegiance to a government or an authority not recognised by the Detaining Power.

4. Persons who accompany the armed forces without actually being members thereof, such as civilian members of military aircraft crews, war correspondents, supply contractors, members of labour units or of services responsible for the welfare of the armed forces, provided that they have received authorisation from the armed forces which they accompany.

5. Members of crews, including masters, pilots and apprentices, of the merchant marine and the crews of civil aircraft of the Parties to the conflict, who do not benefit by more favourable treatment under any other provisions of international law.

---

15 Boothby William H., 2012, *The Law of Targeting*, Oxford: Oxford University Press, p. 312.

16 Dinstein Yoram, 2010, *The Conduct of Hostilities under the Law of International Armed Conflict*, Cambridge: Cambridge University Press, p. 60.

6. Inhabitants of a non-occupied territory who, on the approach of the enemy, spontaneously take up arms to resist the invading forces, without having had time to form themselves into regular armed units, provided they carry arms openly and respect the laws and customs of war.

The above categories of personnel who are at sea and who are wounded, sick or shipwrecked, shall be respected and protected in all circumstances. Such persons shall be treated humanely and cared for by the Parties to the conflict in whose power they may be, without any adverse distinction founded on sex, race, nationality, religion, political opinions, or any other similar criteria. Any attempts upon their lives, or violence to their persons, shall be strictly prohibited; in particular, they shall not be murdered or exterminated, subjected to torture or biological experiments; they shall not wilfully be left without medical assistance and care, nor shall conditions exposing them to contagion or infection be created. Only urgent medical reasons will authorise priority in the order of treatment to be administered. Women shall be treated with all consideration due to their sex.

The wounded, sick and shipwrecked must be respected and protected in all circumstances and wherever they are.[17] The term "shipwreck" means shipwreck from any cause and includes forced landings at sea by or from aircraft. The term "shipwrecked" has been defined as persons, whether military or civilian, who are in peril at sea or in other waters as a result of misfortune affecting them or the vessel or aircraft carrying them and who refrain from any act of hostility. These persons provided that they continue to refrain from any act of hostility, shall continue to be considered shipwrecked during their rescue until they acquire another status under the Geneva Conventions or AP I.[18]

The 1977 AP I Provisions for Wounded and Sick: AP I has several provisions regarding the wounded, sick, and shipwrecked. These provisions have generally not been discussed because the Indian Government is not a party to AP I. These provisions, however, are summarised to familiarise personnel of the naval force, in case they are engaged in multinational operations or are engaged in armed conflict against the states that are parties to AP I.

17 The Second Geneva Convention of 1949, Articles 5 and 12(1); and Article 10(1), 1977 AP I.

18 Article 8(b), 1977 AP I.

Article 12 of AP I elaborates upon the protections afforded to the wounded, sick, and shipwrecked. For example, AP I protects certain civilian medical units. The obligations in AP I also cover both combatants and civilians. To apply AP I, Article 8 of AP I defines "wounded" and "sick" to include persons "whether military or civilian" and "maternity cases, new-born babies and other persons who may be in need of immediate medical assistance or care, such as the infirm or expectant mothers, and who refrain from any act of hostility."

Article 25 of AP I has a few provisions that are intended to expand upon the protection afforded to medical transports. For example, under AP I, the respect and protection of medical aircraft of a party to the conflict in and over land areas physically controlled by friendly forces or in and over sea areas not physically controlled by an adverse party are not dependent on any agreement with an adverse party. Similarly, the protection of small craft described in Article 27 of the Geneva Convention II is afforded, even if the notification envisaged by that Article has not been made.

Articles 32-34 of AP I are intended to help families know the fate of their relatives. For example, as soon as circumstances and the relations between adverse parties permit, the States that are Parties to AP I in whose territories graves may be shall conclude agreements: (i) to facilitate access to gravesites by relatives of the deceased and by representatives of official Graves Registration Services and to regulate the practical arrangements for such access; (ii) to protect and maintain such gravesites permanently; and (iii) to facilitate the return of the remains of the deceased and personal effects to the home country upon its request or, unless that country objects, upon the request of the next of kin.

In addition to these treaties, customary international law is an important source of law applicable to maritime operations due to the extensive development of naval warfare law by state practice and accompanying judicial opinions.[19] Customary rules have the advantage that they do not require any express act of ratification or further acceptance by States. The following are the advantages of customary rules.

- The customary rules of IHL bind all those who participate in armed conflict, whether they are parties to a specific treaty or not. They bind all belligerents on both sides of a conflict.

19 Krask James, David Letts, Raul "Pete" Pedrozo, Wolff Heintschel von Heinegg, James Farrant, Gurpreet S. Khurana, Yurika Ishii, and Koki Sat (ed.), The Newport Manual on the Law of Naval Warfare, *International Law Studies*, Vol. 101, 2023, pp. 250, at p. 8.

- Customary rules are not restricted in their field of application. Many of them apply to all forms of conflict, whether international or non-international.

- Customary rules fill the gaps that exist in the treaty rules applicable in non-international armed conflicts, including targeting, proportionality and precautions in attack.

- They also greatly strengthen the weaker areas of treaty law, such as the protection of civilians and civilian property in times of internal armed conflict.

- The customary rules of IHL are particularly important and relevant to regions prone to situations of armed violence and countries that have a weak record of ratification of IHL treaties.

The International Committee of the Red Cross (1988) has provided seven basic rules containing the crux of the law of armed conflict.[20] These rules are based on the principle of distinction that civilians should never be specifically made a target and combatants have to abide by certain limitations in choosing the means and methods of warfare.

1. Persons *hors de combat* (those out of combat, taken prisoner of war, or injured) and those who do not take a direct part in hostilities are entitled to respect for their lives and their moral and physical integrity. They shall in all circumstances be protected and treated humanely without any adverse distinction.

2. It is forbidden to kill or injure an enemy who surrenders or who is hors de combat.

3. The wounded and sick shall be collected and cared for by the party to the conflict which has them in its power. Protection also covers medical personnel, establishments, transports and equipment. The emblem of the Red Cross or the Red Crescent is the sign of such protection and must be respected.

4. Captured combatants and civilians under the authority of an adverse party are entitled to respect for their lives, dignity, personal rights and convictions. They shall be protected against all acts of violence and reprisals. They shall have the right to correspond

20 Basic rules of international humanitarian law in armed conflicts, Geneva: International Committee of the Red Cross, December 31, 1988.

with their families and to receive relief.

5. Everyone shall be entitled to benefit from fundamental judicial guarantees. No one shall be held responsible for an act he has not committed. No one shall be subjected to physical or mental torture, corporal punishment or cruel or degrading treatment.

6. Parties to a conflict and members of their armed forces do not have an unlimited choice of methods and means of warfare. It is prohibited to employ weapons or methods of warfare of a nature that causes unnecessary losses or excessive suffering.

7. Parties to a conflict shall at all times distinguish between the civilian population and combatants in order to spare the civilian population and property. Neither the civilian population as such nor civilian persons shall be the object of attack. Attacks shall be directed solely against military objectives.

Hospital Ships

Hospital ships, including military hospital ships and coastal rescue craft, while operating in compliance with Geneva Conventions, enjoy special protection and cannot be attacked, sunk or captured under any circumstances. However, in order to prevent a hospital ship from interfering with an enemy's military operations, the enemy may exercise control over it. This control includes searching the hospital ship, dictating its course, putting a commissioner on board, detaining it, or controlling its use of communications equipment.[21] The search ensures that the hospital ship is operating in compliance with the Geneva Conventions. The enemy may dictate its course by refusing help, ordering it off, or determining its direction and speed. The purpose of a commissioner on board is to ensure that the hospital ship follows the orders given to it. The enemy may detain a hospital ship, but only under exceptional circumstances, and this detention may not exceed 7 days. Hospital ships are forbidden to possess or use secret codes in communication equipment.

A hospital ship, its crew and the medical personnel assigned to it are exempt from capture. These medical personnel are treated in a fundamentally different fashion than other medical personnel. The reason for this is that exempting a hospital ship from capture without exempting its crew and

21 Articles 22-35, GC II (1949 Geneva Convention II for the Amelioration of the Condition of the Wounded, Sick, and Shipwrecked Members of Armed Forces at Sea); and Articles 22 and 23, AP I.

personnel would prevent it from carrying out its mission and would turn it into a mere derelict. The exemption from capture extends throughout the period the crew and personnel are assigned to the ship, whether or not they happen to be on board at the time they fall into enemy hands. Similarly, their immunity from capture may not be suspended even if there happens not to be any wounded or sick on board. Medical personnel captured while serving aboard warships or in situations other than serving aboard hospital ships can be retained by the enemy. The wounded and sick aboard hospital ships or other ships become prisoners of war if captured, but the belligerent capturing them must be able to care for them before moving them.

Hospital ships may be as big or as small as a nation wishes to make them, although, for the comfort and safety of the patients on board, the GC II recommends that they be over 2,000 tons.[22] Ships may be built specifically as hospital ships or merchant ships may be converted into hospital ships. However, once a merchant ship becomes a hospital ship, it must remain a hospital ship throughout the hostilities. Advance notification of 10 days is required before employment of a hospital ship.[23]

Article 43 of GC II lays down specifications on the marking of hospital ships and small crafts. All exterior surfaces of hospital ships should be white. One or more dark red crosses, as large as possible, are to be painted and displayed on each side of the hull and the horizontal surfaces, so placed as to afford the greatest possible visibility from the sea and the air. All hospital ships must hoist their national flag and further, if they belong to a neutral State, the flag of the Party to the conflict whose direction they have accepted. A white flag with a red cross should be flown at the mainmast as high as possible. Lifeboats of hospital ships, coastal lifeboats and small craft used by the medical service should be painted white with dark red crosses, prominently displayed. They must comply with the identification

22 This provision (Article 26) was included in GC II of 1949 because of UK's announcement during World War II that it would refuse to recognize as protected any hospital ship of less than 3,000 tons. This announcement was in response to the large number of small rescue craft used by Germany to pick up downed pilots in the immediate vicinity of Britain's coastal defences at a time when invasion by Germany was thought imminent.

23 During World War I it had been the practice of Great Britain to move merchant ships in and out of medical service, prompting Germany to torpedo a number of them. Also, there were instances of hasty conversion of merchant ships into hospital ships to avoid capture, such as the German ship *Rostock* in the besieged port of Bordeaux in 1944. A rule requiring a 10-day advanced notification before employment of a hospital ship should prevent abuses of this sort.

system prescribed for hospital ships. States must take adequate measures for the prevention and repression of any abuse of the distinctive signs.[24]

If hospital ships are misused for military purposes or act in any other way contrary to their obligations, in particular by clearly resisting an order to stop, to turn away or follow a distinct code, they lose their protected status. The protection shall cease after due warning has been given.[25] The fact that the crews of ships or sick bays are armed for the maintenance of order, for their defence or that of the sick and wounded, would not deprive a hospital ship of protection.[26] If after due warning a hospital ship persists in breaking a condition of its exemption, it renders itself liable to capture or other necessary measures to enforce compliance.[27]

Medical Aircraft

Collection and evacuation of the wounded, sick and shipwrecked, as well as the transport of medical personnel and equipment, are a vital part of efforts to mitigate the suffering associated with armed conflict. Sometimes, the fastest means of carrying out these humanitarian tasks is by aircraft including helicopters. In practice, helicopters are particularly important for removing the wounded, sick and shipwrecked and are an integral component of military medical capabilities. Article 39 of the Second Geneva Convention confers protection on medical aircraft but subjects that protection to relatively stringent criteria.[28]

Article 39 provides that medical aircraft exclusively employed for the removal of wounded, sick and shipwrecked, and for the transport of medical personnel and equipment, may not be the object of attack. Such aircraft shall be respected by the Parties to the conflict, while flying at

24 Articles 43-45, GC II.

25 Article 34, GC II.

26 Article 35 (1), GC II.

27 Doswald-Beck Louise (ed.),1995, *San Remo Manual on International Law Applicable to Armed Conflict at Sea*, International Institute of Humanitarian Law, Cambridge: Cambridge University Press, pp. 253, at para 50.

28 The reason for the stringency is that, at the time of drafting the Geneva Conventions, the precise nature of an enemy aircraft was very difficult to ascertain from a distance. Moreover, ever since the advent of aviation, there has been a concern that medical aircraft may be used as a cover for acquiring information of military value. Dormann Knut, Liesbeth Lijnzaad, Marco Sassoli and Philip Spoerri, (ed), 2017, *Updated Commentary on the Second Geneva Convention of 1949*, ICRC, Cambridge: Cambridge University Press, para 2568, p. 901.

heights, at times and on routes specifically agreed upon between the Parties to the conflict concerned. The aircraft shall be marked with the distinctive emblem,[29] together with their national colours, on their lower, upper and lateral surfaces. They shall be provided with any other markings or means of identification which may be agreed upon between the Parties to the conflict upon the outbreak or during hostilities. Unless agreed otherwise, flights over enemy or enemy-occupied territory are prohibited. Medical aircraft shall obey every summons to alight on land or water. In the event of having thus to alight, the aircraft with its occupants may continue its flight after examination, if any. In the event of alighting involuntarily on land or water in enemy or enemy-occupied territory, the wounded, sick and shipwrecked, as well as the crew of the aircraft shall be prisoners of war. As prisoners of war, they shall be entitled to protection under the third Geneva Convention of 1949.

Legal Manuals

San Remo Manual and The Newport Manual on the Law of Naval Warfare are two major compilations and interpretations of the legal framework in the maritime domain. In addition, certain secondary sources provide further guidelines and insight into the application of IHL in naval and submarine warfare.[30]

San Remo Manual

The 1994 San Remo Manual is another source of the law of naval warfare, albeit a non-binding, drafted by an international group of specialists in international law and naval experts. It is a contemporary restatement - together with some progressive development - of the law applicable to

29 Article 41 of the Second Geneva Convention provides, "Under the direction of the competent military authority, the emblem of the red cross on a white ground shall be displayed on the flags, armlets and on all equipment (including aircraft) employed in the Medical Service. Nevertheless, in the case of countries which already use as emblem, in place of the red cross, the red crescent or the red lion and sun on a white ground, these emblems are also recognized by the terms of the present Convention."

30 Some of these secondary sources are: (i) The Federal Republic of Germany Ministry of Defence Manual, Humanitarian Law in Armed Conflict (1992); (ii) The UK Manual on The Law of Armed Conflict (2004); (iii) Fleck Dieter (2008), The Handbook of International Humanitarian Law, Oxford University Press; (iv) United States of America, Department of Defence, Law of War Manual (2016); (v) The US Commander's Handbook on the Law of Naval Operations (March 2022); and (vi) New Zealand, Manual of Armed Forces Law (2019), DM 69.

armed conflicts at sea.[31] The San Remo Manual has met a good response as a contemporary restatement of the principles and rules of international law applicable to armed conflict at sea. The Manual containing 183 rules is divided into six substantive Parts which cover the following topics:

Part I General Provisions,

Part II Regions of Operations,

Part III Basic Rules and Target Discrimination,

Part IV Methods and Means of Warfare at Sea,

Part V Measures Short of Attack: Interception, Visit, Search, Diversion and Capture, and

Part VI Protected Persons, Medical Transports and Medical Aircraft.

It contains various provisions regarding the non-forcible uses of ocean space by warships.

According to Wolf Heintschel (2016), many provisions of the San Remo Manual are but a compromise between the differing view within the group of international lawyers and naval experts who drafted it, and some of its provisions are far from perfect. For instance, the law of neutrality is one of the most disputed aspects of public international law. The drafters of the Manual have been heavily criticised for having adopted a rather traditional approach to the law of maritime neutrality. [32] It is now nearly 30 years since the project that resulted in the publication of the San Remo Manual completed its work. During the period since publication, there have been several significant issues impacting the law of naval warfare that have emerged, such as the impact of new technologies in weapons and communications, the impact of the cyber warfare domain and there are also some mistakes that were included in the San Remo Manual that warrant correction. The San Remo Manual also neglects to consider, in any detail, how the law of naval warfare might be applied in non-international armed conflict. The experience of the armed conflict between Sri Lankan forces

31 Doswald-Beck Louise (ed.),1995, San Remo Manual on International Law Applicable to Armed Conflict at Sea, International Institute of Humanitarian Law, Cambridge: Cambridge University Press, p. 253.

32 Heinegg Wolf Heintschel von, The Current State of the Law of Naval Warfare: A Fresh Look at the San Remo Manual, International Law Studies, Vol. 82, 2006, pp. 269-296.

and the maritime forces of the Liberation Tigers of Tamil Eelam indicates that consideration of that aspect of the law is certainly warranted.[33]

The Newport Manual on the Law of Naval Warfare

The Stockton Centre for International Law at the US Naval War College has recently brought Newport Manual on the Law of Naval Warfare, published as a special volume of International Law Studies (ILS).[34] The Manual on the Law of Naval Warfare reflects the law as it exists (*lex lata*); that is, the prevailing rules governing international armed conflict at sea as States have recognised and employed them in the past and present. The views presented in the Newport Manual reflect the personal views of the authors/ editors. It does not reflect the official policy or position of any government, ministry of defence, university, or institution. The Newport Manual is a work of scholarship produced by the authors in their capacity, albeit benefiting from their operational law experience in service in the armed forces.

This Manual tries to bring together theoretical and practical aspects of maritime operations, discussed in the next eight chapters, that would be applicable in future maritime operations.

A table of IHL treaties is placed at Annexure I to this chapter. The legal regime of the Oceans is placed at Annexure II.

33 Letts David, International Law and Armed Conflicts at Sea: The San Remo Manual – now is the time for a LOTE! *Australian Naval Review*, Issue 1, June 2020, available at: https://navalinstitute.com.au/international-law-and-armed-conflicts-at-sea/.

34 Kraska James, David Letts, Raul "Pete" Pedrozo, Wolff Heintschel von Heinegg; James Farrant, Gurpreet S. Khurana, Yurika Ishii, and Koki Sat (ed.), *International Law Studies*, Volume 101, 2023, p. 265.

Annexure I

TABLE OF TREATIES

The following are the main law of armed conflict or IHL treaties in chronological order of adoption:

1864 Geneva Convention for the amelioration of the condition of the wounded in armies in the field.

1868 Declaration of St. Petersburg (prohibiting the use of certain projectiles in wartime).

1899 The Hague Conventions respecting the laws and customs of war on land and the adaptation to maritime warfare of the principles of the 1864 Geneva Convention.

1906 Review and development of the 1864 Geneva Convention for the amelioration of the condition of the wounded in armies in the field.

1907 Review of The Hague Conventions of 1899 and adoption of new Conventions.

The 1907 Hague Convention No. VI Relating to the Status of Enemy Merchant Ships at the Outbreak of Hostilities

The 1907 Hague Convention No. VII Relating to the Conversion of Merchant Ships into War-ships

The 1907 Convention No. VIII Relative to the Laying of Automatic Submarine Contact Mines.

The 1907 Hague Convention No. IX Concerning Bombardments by Naval Forces in Time of War

The 1907 Hague Convention No. XI Relative to Certain Restrictions with Regard to the Exercise of the Right of Capture in Naval War

The 1907 Hague Convention No. XIII Concerning the Rights and Duties of Neutral Powers in Naval War

1925 Geneva Protocol for the prohibition of the use in war of asphyxiating, poisonous or other gases and of bacteriological methods of warfare.

1929 Two Geneva Conventions: 1. Review and development of the 1906 Geneva Convention, for the amelioration of the condition of the wounded in armies in the field; and 2. Geneva Convention relating to the Treatment of Prisoners of War (new).

1949 the four Geneva Conventions:[35]

> I Amelioration of the condition of the wounded and sick in armed forces in the field
>
> II Amelioration of the condition of wounded, sick and shipwrecked members of armed forces at sea
>
> III Treatment of prisoners of war
>
> IV Protection of civilian persons in time of war.[36]

1954 The Hague Convention for the protection of cultural property in the event of armed conflict.

1969 Vienna Convention on the Law of Treaties.

1972 Convention on the prohibition of the development, production and stockpiling of bacteriological (biological) and toxic weapons and on their destruction (BWC).

1976 UN Convention on the Prohibition of Military or Any Other Hostile Use of Environmental Modification Techniques (ENMOD).

35 In 1949 the former Geneva Conventions were revised: the Geneva Convention of 1929 for the Relief of the Wounded and Sick in Armies in the Field; the Xth Hague Convention of 1907 for the Adaptation to Maritime War of the Principles of the Geneva Convention; and 1929 Convention on the Treatment of Prisoners of war. Further, there was an urgent need for a Convention for the Protection of Civilians, the absence of which had, during the world conflict, led to grievous consequences. The main principles laid down in the 1864 Convention and maintained by the later Geneva Conventions are: (i) relief to the wounded without any distinction as to nationality; (ii) neutrality (inviolability) of medical personnel and medical establishments and units; and (iii) the distinctive sign of the Red Cross on a white ground.

36 The Second World War (1939-1945) saw civilians and military personnel killed in equal numbers, as against a ratio of 1:10 in the First World War. In 1949 the international community responded to those tragic figures, and more particularly to the terrible effects the war had on civilians, by revising the Conventions then in force and adopting a new instrument: the Fourth Geneva Convention for the Protection of Civilians.

1977 Two Protocols addition to the four 1949 Geneva Conventions, strengthen the protection of victims of international (Protocol I) and non-international (Protocol II) armed conflicts.

1980 Convention on prohibitions or restrictions on the use of certain conventional weapons which may be deemed to be excessively injurious or to have indiscriminate effects (CCW), which includes:

- Protocol I of 1980 on non-detectable fragments.
- Protocol II of 1980 on prohibitions or restrictions on the use of mines, booby traps and other devices.
- Protocol III of 1980 on prohibitions or restrictions on the use of incendiary weapons.
- Protocol IV of 1995 relating to blinding laser weapons.
- Revised Protocol of 1996 on prohibitions or restrictions on the use of mines, booby traps and other devices.
- Amendment of 2001 relating to Article I of the CCW of 1980.
- Protocol V of 2003 on Explosive Remnants of War.

1982 United Nations Convention on the Law of the Sea.

1993 Convention on the prohibition of the development, production, stockpiling and use of chemical weapons and on their destruction (CWC).

1997 Convention on the prohibition of the use, stockpiling, production and transfer of anti-personnel mines and their destruction.

1998 Rome Statute of the International Criminal Court.

1999 Protocol to the 1954 Convention on Cultural Property.

2000 Optional Protocol to the Convention on the Rights of the Child (CRC) on the involvement of children in armed conflict.

2004 Rules of Customary International Humanitarian Law released by the ICRC.

2005 third Protocols Additional to the four 1949 Geneva Conventions Relating to Adoption of Additional Protective Emblem.

2008 Convention on Prohibition of the Use, Development and Destruction of Cluster Munitions.

2014 Arms Trade Treaty.

2021 The Treaty on the Prohibition of Nuclear Weapons.

Annexure II: The Legal Regimes of the Oceans

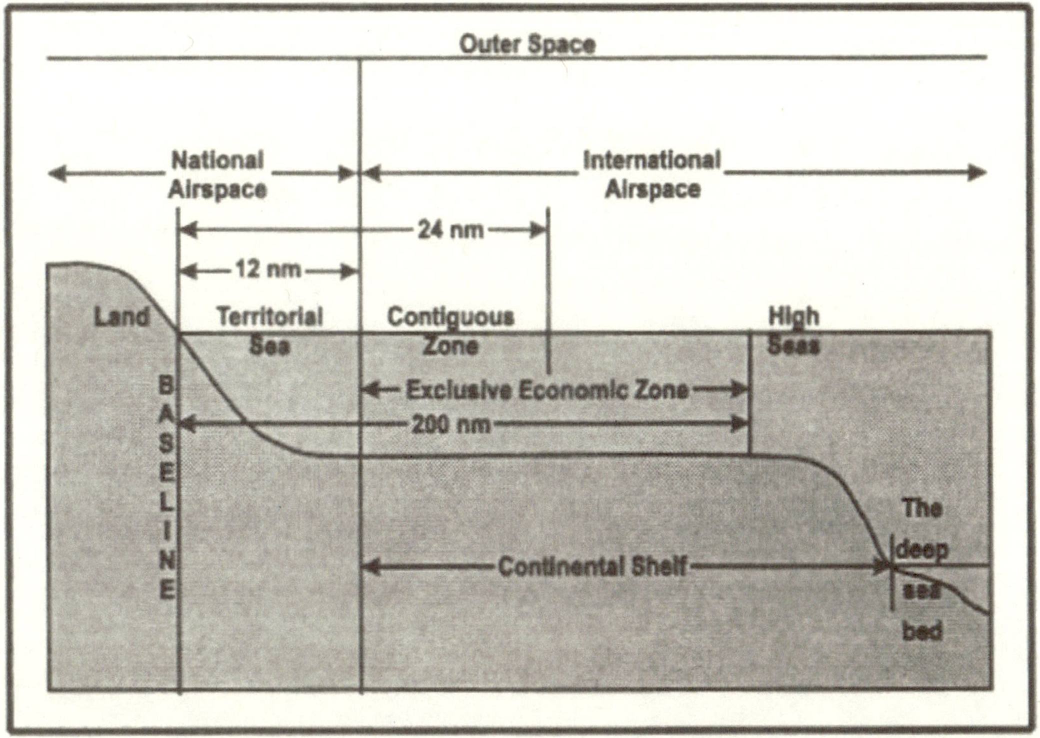

II

Winds and Sails

Maritime Operations: Means and Methods

The term "means and methods of naval warfare" reflects the difference that exists between the weapons that are used in warfare (means) and the tactics and strategies (methods) that are employed to affect the enemy adversely. While the division between "means" and "methods" may sometimes be confusing; generally, "means" are weapons, such as missiles, mines, torpedoes, and gun projectiles. The term "methods of warfare" is used in different contexts across the law of armed conflict (LOAC), and is usually understood as how the means are used.

The guiding principle in a consideration of the rules governing the weapons and methods of naval warfare is that in the absence of restrictions imposed either by custom or by convention, belligerents are permitted in their mutual relations to use any means in the conduct of hostilities. The lawfulness of the weapons and methods of war must be determined not only by the express prohibitions contained in specific rules of custom and convention but also by those prohibitions laid down in the general principles of the law of war. The general principles of the law of war are contained in distinction, proportionality and unnecessary suffering. In addition, the principle of humanity forbids the employment of any kind or degree of force that is unnecessary for the purpose(s) of war; the force which needlessly or unnecessarily causes human suffering and physical destruction is prohibited. There is also the principle forbidding the resort to treacherous means (perfidy) in the waging of hostilities.[1]

1 Tucker Robert W., The Law of War and Neutrality at Sea, *International Law Studies*, Vol. 50, 1955, pp. 45-150.

Limitations on Means - Prohibited Weapons

The employment of weapons designed to cause superfluous injury or unnecessary suffering is prohibited. Some weapons (e.g., poisoned projectiles) are unlawful per se. Others may be rendered unlawful by alteration (e.g., coating ammunition with poison). Certain means of warfare have been prohibited from use on the battlefield, either because they are regarded as causing unnecessary suffering or superfluous injury or for policy reasons. These include poison, chemical weapons, biological (or bacteriological) weapons, munitions containing fragments not detectable by X-ray, and blinding laser weapons. Any lawful weapon is capable of being used for an unlawful purpose when it is directed against noncombatants, civilians, and other protected persons and property. Today, directed energy weapons (DEWs) are a permissible means of warfare if they are lawfully employed.[2]

There are no rules of customary or conventional international law prohibiting states from employing nuclear weapons in armed conflict. In the absence of an express prohibition, the use of nuclear weapons against enemy combatants and other military objectives is not unlawful.

Indiscriminate Weapons

Weapons which by their nature are incapable of being directed specifically against military objectives, and therefore put civilians and noncombatants at equivalent risk, are forbidden due to their indiscriminate effect. Examples of weapons incapable of discrimination include drifting armed contact mines, and long-range unguided missiles (e.g., the German V-1 and V-2 rockets and Japanese uncontrolled balloon-borne bombs used during World War II). Torpedoes must be designed to sink or otherwise become harmless when they have missed their intended target.[3] This rule

---

2 Two examples of Directed Energy Weapons (DEWs) are the US HELIOS (High Energy Laser with Integrated Optical-dazzler and Surveillance) and the Russian 5P-42 Filin. DEWs are electromagnetic systems capable of converting chemical or electrical energy to radiated energy and focusing it on a target, resulting in physical damage. States are developing numerous types of directed energy weapons that include high-energy lasers and high-powered microwave weapons. Directed energy weapons use concentrated electromagnetic energy, rather than kinetic energy, to incapacitate, damage, disable, or destroy enemy equipment, facilities, and/or personnel. Kraska James et. al., (ed.), 2023, Newport Manual on the Law of Naval Warfare, *International Law Studies*, Vol. 101, p. 107.

3 Torpedoes must be designed to become harmless upon completion of their propulsion run, such as by sinking to the bottom. Modern torpedoes may be equipped with

is based upon the premise that a torpedo that misses its target becomes a hazard to innocent shipping in the same manner as a free-floating mine.[4]

Booby traps and other delayed-action devices are not unlawful, provided they are not designed to cause unnecessary suffering or are employed indiscriminately. Since India has not signed the 1997 Anti-Personnel Mine Ban Treaty, anti-personnel mines can be employed to deny, for example, the use of shore facilities in a port.[5]

Incendiary Weapons

The 1980 Conventional Weapons Convention, Protocol III regulates the use of incendiary weapons. An "incendiary weapon" is defined as "any weapon or munition which is primarily designed to set fire to objects or to cause burn injury to persons through the action of flame, heat, or combination thereof, produced by a chemical reaction of a substance delivered on the target." Incendiary weapons can take the form of flame throwers, fougasses, shells, rockets, grenades, mines, bombs and other containers of incendiary substances. It is prohibited to make the civilian population, individual civilians or civilian objects the object of attack by incendiary weapons. It is also prohibited to make any military objective located within a concentration of civilians the object of attack by air-delivered incendiary weapons. It is further prohibited to make any military objective located within a concentration of civilians the object of attack using incendiary weapons other than air-delivered incendiary weapons,

autonomous fire-and-forget operation or wire-guide capability to allow post-launch monitoring and updates via the submarine combat system.

4 Hague Convention No. VIII (1907). Articles 1 through 3 of the Convention state as follows: Article I. It is forbidden: (i) To lay unanchored automatic contact mines, except when they are so constructed as to become harmless one hour at most after the person who laid them ceases to control them; (ii) To lay anchored automatic contact mines which do not become harmless as soon as they have broken loose from their moorings; (iii) To use torpedoes which do not become harmless when they have missed their mark. Article 2: It is forbidden to lay automatic contact mines off the coast and ports of the enemy, with the sole object of intercepting commercial shipping. Article 3: When anchored automatic contact mines are employed, every possible precaution must be taken for the security of peaceful shipping. The belligerents undertake to do their utmost to render these mines harmless within a limited time, and, should they cease to be under surveillance, to notify the danger zones as soon as military exigencies permit, by a notice addressed to ship-owners, which must also be communicated to the Governments through the diplomatic channel.

5 The Convention on the Prohibition of the Use, Stockpiling, Production and Transfer of Anti-Personnel Mines and on their Destruction of 1997, known informally as the Ottawa Treaty.

except when such military objective is separated from the concentration of civilians. All feasible precautions must be taken to limit the incendiary effects to the military objective of minimising, incidental loss of civilian life, injury to civilians and damage to civilian objects.

Cluster Munitions

The 2008 Convention on Cluster Munitions (CCM), prohibits the use, development, production, acquisition, stockpiling, retention, or transfer of cluster munitions. Since India is not a party to this convention, cluster munitions may be used by the naval forces.

Methods – Permitted and Prohibited

Protective Signs

Certain signs, signals, and symbols reflect a status that receives special protection under the law of armed conflict. These signs may not be improperly used. They may not be used: (i) While engaging in attacks; (ii) In order to shield, favour, or protect one's military operations; and (iii) To impede enemy military operations. Their use may be improper even when that use does not involve killing or wounding. They may not be used to facilitate espionage (except for signs, emblems, or uniforms of a neutral or non-belligerent State). The prohibited acts are unlawful because they undermine the effectiveness of protective signs, signals, and symbols and thereby jeopardise the safety of noncombatants and civilians, as well as the immunity of protected structures and activities. For example, using a ship, ambulance or medical aircraft marked with the Red Cross or Red Crescent to carry armed combatants, weapons, or ammunition with which to attack or elude enemy forces is prohibited. The use of the white flag to gain a military advantage over the enemy is unlawful.

False flags

The term "false flag" probably originated in naval warfare dating back to the 16th century. A warship might occasionally fly the flag of a neutral – or even enemy – nation to get as close as possible to a hostile warship before opening fire. The practice was considered advantageous in the military sense in an age when the range of warships' cannons was quite limited. It was highly desirable to close with an enemy ship to disable it and, if possible, board it to take it as a prize. As a tool in the hands of the weaker party in a conflict, it could also help to even the odds. Such conduct, and other similar acts of deception were not considered illegal, provided the correct flag was flown during actual combat. This practice continued into both World Wars.[6]

Unlike land and air warfare, naval warfare permits the use of false flags or military emblems.[7] Under the customary international law of naval warfare, it is permissible to fly false colours, including those of a neutral State, from a belligerent warship or naval auxiliary and to disguise their outward appearance, or employ other methods and means in other ways to deceive the enemy into believing the vessel is of neutral nationality or is other than a military ship. It is unlawful for a warship to go into action without first showing her true colours. Use of neutral flags, insignia, or uniforms during an actual armed engagement at sea is forbidden. The flag of the United Nations and the letters UN must not be used in armed conflict for any purpose without the authorisation of the United Nations. Given the technological developments, the use of false flags has almost become a negligible issue. Before opening fire, however, the true flag shall always be displayed.[8]

Prevention of Misuse of the Distinctive Emblem

Article 45 of the Second Geneva Convention places a positive obligation on States Parties to take the necessary measures to prevent and repress any abuse of the distinctive signs provided for under Article 43. Article 45 is intended to prevent misuse of the distinctive signs displayed on ships, lifeboats and coastal rescue craft (including aircraft and helicopters). States are required to prevent and repress such abuses at all times. Consequently, the measures taken must address abuses both in times of peace and in times of armed conflict. Failure to regulate the use of distinctive emblems in peacetime may contribute to abuse in situations of armed conflict. Article 45 requires States to take the necessary measures if their legislation is not already adequate. Therefore, apart from the administrative measures

6 For example, in 1914 the German light cruiser SMS Emden, possessing a distinctive three-funnel silhouette, rigged up a fourth (dummy) funnel to make herself look more like a British light cruiser of equivalent class. In 1941 the German commerce raider Kormoran used the call-sign and flag of a Dutch merchantman to tempt the Australian cruiser HMAS Sydney to approach as close as possible. This reduced Sydney's advantages of superior gun range and heavier armour; Kormoran hoisted the German battle ensign on opening fire, resulting in Sydney's loss with all 645 of its crew.

7 Article 39, paragraph 3, 1977 AP I.

8 Fleck Dieter (ed.). 2008. *The Handbook of International Humanitarian Law*, Oxford: Oxford University Press, paragraph 1008, p. 494.

incumbent on the competent authorities, each country must enact legislation to prohibit and punish misuse of the emblems at all times.

Ruses and Perfidy

Ruses of war are permissible in naval warfare. The law of armed conflict or IHL permits deceiving the enemy through ruses of war intended to mislead the enemy, deter the enemy from taking action, or induce the enemy to act recklessly, provided the ruses do not constitute perfidy or otherwise violate the rules of international law applicable to armed conflict. Ruses of war are methods, resources, and techniques that can be used to convey false information or deny information to opposing forces. Ruses (or, tricks) of war may include: (i) Physical, technical, or administrative means, such as electronic warfare measures; (ii) Flares, smoke, and chaff; (iii) Camouflage; (iv) Deceptive lighting; (v) Dummy ships and other armament; (vi) Decoys; (vii) Simulated forces; (viii) Feigned attacks and withdrawals; (ix) Ambushes; (x) False intelligence information; (xi) Utilisation of enemy codes, passwords, and countersigns; (xii) Transmission of a false position through an automatic identification system or other electronic identification systems, etc.[9] However, Morris (2007)[10] is of the view that the inclusion of "deceptive lighting" on the list of ruses is legally and pragmatically incorrect and amounts to perfidy. Because, instead of simply confusing or misleading the enemy, "deceptive lighting" invites the enemy to think that the combatant enjoys some sort of protected status with regards to international law,"[11]

In modern-day armed conflict, hostile statements made or acts committed to pinning the blame on another party, usually one's adversary, is a recognised tactic of organised warfare. They aim to deceive the enemy to gain a military advantage. As such there is nothing inherently illegal about

9 The Commander's Handbook on the Law of Naval Operations, March 2022, The US Department of Navy/ Marine Corps and Coast Guard, p. 182.

10 Morris Matthew G, *"Hiding Amongst a Crowd" and the Illegality of Deceptive Lighting*, Naval Law Review, Vol. 54, 2007, pp. 235-258.

11 The fact remains that the general principles of armed conflict governing sea are different than those governing armed conflict on land. This is especially true regarding the laws surrounding perfidy at sea, where express provisions of international treaties denote the difference of the rule as applied at sea and on land. Lee Brennan, Deceptive Lighting: Shining a Light on Gaps in the Legal Regime and Accountability for the Law of Armed Conflict at Sea, *Minnesota Journal of International Law*, Vol. 30, No. 2, 2021, pp. 359-393.

them within the framework of IHL.[12] Ruses were first acknowledged in the 1863 Lieber Code. In modern warfare, they are expressly allowed by Article 24 of the 1907 Hague Regulations and Article 37(2) of AP I. The ruses are also recognised as rules of customary IHL. However, to be considered legal such acts must not violate another rule of IHL. In particular, a false flag action must not constitute perfidious or treacherous behaviour.

It is unlawful to injure or kill persons utilising perfidy. Acts of perfidy are acts that invite the confidence of the enemy to lead them to believe that they are entitled to, or are obliged to accord, protected status under the law of armed conflict, with the intent to betray that confidence. Perfidy is prohibited, because it may undermine the protections afforded by the law of war to certain classes of persons and objects; diminish legitimate activities that depend upon trust between hostile forces; and damage the basis for the restoration of peace short of the complete annihilation of one belligerent by another. Feigning surrender and then attacking, feigning an intent to negotiate under a flag of truce and then attacking, and feigning death or incapacitation by wounds or sickness and then attacking are examples of acts of perfidy. While ruses are permitted in war, the use of unlawful deceptions constitutes perfidy and is, therefore, a prohibited war crime.

The acts of perfidy are deceptions designed to invite the confidence of the enemy to lead him to believe that he is entitled to, or is obliged to accord, protected status under the law of armed conflict, with the intent to betray that confidence. Three examples which demonstrate the breach required for

12 For instance, at the beginning of March 2023, Ukraine dismissed as "provocation" a Russian claim that Ukrainian "terrorists" or "sabotage groups" were behind a series of disputed attacks and exchanges of fire in Russia's Kursk and Bryansk regions, near the Ukrainian frontier. Overnight on March 9-10, Russia launched a barrage of 81 missiles against targets all over Ukraine, including six hypersonic missiles labelling them retribution for those earlier attacks. In the week of the first anniversary of the start of Russia's "special military operation" in Ukraine, the Institute for the Study of published a report claiming that Moscow was setting up attacks on Belarusian territory and inside the Moldovan secessionist republic of Transnistria to make it look as though they had been carried out by Ukrainian troops. This would potentially justify Belarus' formal entry into the war on Russia's side. In turn, this would force Ukraine to divert troops and materiel away from the currently "hot" military operations in Donbas towards the northwestern and southwestern frontiers of the country. On February 19, Russia's Ministry of Defence alleged that Ukraine was preparing to stage an unspecified "nuclear incident" on Ukrainian territory with radioactive substances imported from an unnamed European country, in order to blame it on the Kremlin But no evidence supporting such allegations was produced and no such incidents have actually taken place.

an act to be considered perfidious could be (i) Misuse of an internationally protected sign, such as the Red Cross; misuse of protective signs, signals, and symbols in order to injure, kill, or capture the enemy constitutes an act of perfidy. (ii) The feigning of distress through internationally recognised distress signals such as MAYDAY and SOS which evoke the traditional requirement for mariners to aid those in distress at sea; and (iii) The misuse of a flag of truce. A white flag has traditionally indicated a desire to communicate with the enemy and depending upon the situation, to surrender. Thus, the use of a flag of truce or white flag in order to deceive or mislead the enemy, or for any purpose other than to negotiate or surrender, has long been recognised as an act of treachery.[13]

Prohibition of Reprisals

Reprisals against the wounded, sick and shipwrecked persons, the personnel, the vessels or the equipment protected by Article 47 of the Second Geneva Convention are prohibited. Belligerent reprisals are measures taken in the context of an international armed conflict by a Party in reaction to a violation of IHL by an adversary. Such measures may not be carried out for revenge or punishment, but only to put an end to such violations and induce the adversary to comply with the law. Although the acts constituting belligerent reprisals are in principle unlawful, their wrongfulness is precluded because of the particular circumstances in which they are taken, i.e., in response to a violation committed by an adversary.[14]

During the Iran-Iraq war, numerous attacks on civilian objects were reported. In 1984, in a message addressed to the Presidents of the Islamic Republic of Iran and the Republic of Iraq, the UN Secretary-General stated that he was profoundly distressed on learning of the heavy civilian casualties caused by the aerial attack on the town of Banesh on June 5, 1984, ... and the retaliatory and counter-retaliatory attacks that followed on towns in Iran and Iraq. Deliberate military attacks on civilian areas cannot be condoned by the international community. The initiation of such attacks

13 Hall Mary T., False Colours and Dummy Ships: The Use of Ruse in Naval Warfare, *Naval War College Review*, Vol. 42, No. 3, Summer 1989, pp. 52-62.

14 Reprisals may be carried out only as a measure of last resort, when no other lawful measures are available to induce the adversary to respect the law. Reprisals must cease as soon as the adversary again complies with the law. It is recognized that reprisal action must be proportionate to the violation it aims to stop. Dormann Knut, Liesbeth Lijnzaad, Marco Sassoli and Philip Spoerri, (ed), 2017, *Updated Commentary on the Second Geneva Convention of 1949*, ICRC, Cambridge: Cambridge University Press, para 2844.p. 997.

in the past, and the reprisals and counter-reprisals they provoke, have resulted in mounting loss of life and suffering to innocent and defenceless civilian populations. It is imperative that this immediately cease.[15]

Orders or Threats that No Quarter Will Be Given

The prohibition on declaring that no quarter[16] will be given is a long-standing rule of customary international law already codified in Article 23 of the Hague Regulations. An order that no quarter will be given, threatening an adversary therewith or conducting hostilities on this basis is prohibited. State practice establishes this rule as a norm of customary international law applicable in both international and non-international armed conflicts. According to William E. Hall (1895), "The right to kill and wound armed enemies is subordinated to the condition that those enemies shall be able and willing to continue their resistance. It is unnecessary to kill men who are incapacitated by wounds from harming, or who are ready to surrender as prisoners. A belligerent therefore may only kill those enemies whom he is permitted to attack while combat is actually in progress; he may not as a general rule refuse quarter, and he cannot mutilate or maim those who fall into his power."[17] The prohibition is contained in numerous military manuals. Under the legislation of many States, it is an offence to issue an order that no quarter be given. In several cases after the First and Second World Wars, the accused were charged with violating this rule.

Para Descent

Under customary rules of IHL, parachutists descending from disabled aircraft may not be attacked while in the air,[18] unless they engage in

15 UN Secretary-General, Message dated June 9, 1984 addressed to the Presidents of the Islamic Republic of Iran and the Republic of Iraq, UN Doc. S/16611, June 11, 1984.

16 The term may originate from an order by the commander of a victorious army that they will not quarter (house) captured enemy combatants. Therefore, none can be taken prisoner and all enemy combatants must be killed.

17 Hall William Edward, 1895, *A Treatise on International Law*, London: The Clarendon Press, pp. 791, at pp. 413-414.

18 Article 42, the 1977 Additional Protocol I. Article 20 of the 1923 Hague Rules of Air Warfare provides: "In the event of an aircraft being disabled, the persons trying to escape by means of parachutes must not be attacked during their descent." Australia's Commanders' Guide (1994) provides, "Aircrew who have bailed out of a damaged aircraft are to be considered as *hors de combat* and should not be attacked during their descent. However, should the parachutist land in enemy territory he must be given an opportunity to surrender before being made the object of an attack unless it is apparent that he is engaged in a hostile act."

combatant acts while descending. Upon reaching the ground, such parachutists must be provided an opportunity to surrender. Airborne troops, special warfare infiltrators, and intelligence agents parachuting into combat areas or behind enemy lines are not so protected and may be attacked in the air and on the ground. Such personnel may not be attacked if they indicate on time their intention to surrender.[19]

Concept of Attack in Naval Warfare

The definition of 'attack' under IHL is codified in article 49 of 1977 AP I. According to the definition, which also reflects customary IHL, "Attacks means acts of violence against the adversary, whether in offence or defence".[20] An 'attack' under IHL, can only exist within the conduct of hostilities. The term 'combat action' differs from 'attack' as the former refers to a host of activities against the adversary, either in offence or defence, and includes the concept of attacks. The act of 'attack' must take place within the context of the conduct of hostilities, including violence and be carried out either in offence or in defence. For purposes of the law of naval warfare, an attack is an act of violence against the adversary, whether carried out by conventional, kinetic means (such as bombs, missiles, and torpedoes), or by non-kinetic means like cyber; if they result, or are designed to result, in damage, destruction, injury, or death.

Legal Framework for An Attack

The treaties which apply to naval targeting and lawful objects of attack or capture are the following: Hague Convention (IV) Respecting the Laws and Customs of War on Land (1907);[21] Hague Convention (VI) Relating to

19 Withholding attack against airmen descending from a disabled aircraft had hardened into customary international law. This provision has been adopted in Article 42 of the 1977 Additional Protocol I. Airborne troops are not protected by this Article. Sabel Robbie, Chivalry in the Air? Article 42 of the 1977 Protocol I to the Geneva Conventions, *International Law Studies*, Vol. 75, 2000, pp. 439-453.

20 The 1977 AP I, Article 49, para 3, further provides, "The provisions of this section apply to any land, air or sea warfare which may affect the civilian population, individual civilians or civilian objects on land. They further apply to all attacks from the sea or from the air against objectives on land but do not otherwise affect the rules of international law applicable in armed conflict at sea or in the air."

21 The Hague Convention IV, concerning land warfare, is also applicable to naval warfare because it states basic principles equally applicable to naval targeting. For example, it prohibits the employment of "arms projectiles, or material calculated to cause unnecessary suffering."

the Status of Enemy Merchant Ships at the Outbreak of Hostilities (1907); Hague Convention (VII) Relating to the Conversion of Merchant Ships into War-Ships (1907); Hague Convention (VIII) Relative to the Laying of Automatic Submarine Contact Mines (1907); Hague Convention (IX) Concerning Bombardment by Naval Forces in Time of War (1907); Hague Convention (XI) Relative to Certain Restrictions with Regard to the Exercise of the Right of Capture in Naval War (1907); and Geneva Convention (II) for the Amelioration of the Condition of the Wounded, Sick and Shipwrecked Members of Armed Forces at Sea, 1949. Because of technological advancement in the field of weapons and methods, for instance, cyber-attack; some of the treaties mentioned above are less applicable to contemporary naval targeting than when they were introduced.[22]

Customary Principles

The customary principle of targeting law is based on the concept that the right of belligerents to adopt means of injuring the enemy is not unlimited. A group of general and fundamental principles are central in pursuing this aim to limit the effects of armed conflicts: the principle of necessity, humanity, proportionality, distinction and chivalry. Military necessity has traditionally been seen as permitting a State involved in an armed conflict to use 'only that degree and kind of force, not otherwise prohibited by the law of armed conflict, that is required to achieve the legitimate purpose of the conflict, namely the complete or partial submission of the enemy at the earliest possible moment with the minimum expenditure of life and resources.'[23] The principle of humanity is linked to that of military necessity. It forbids the infliction of suffering, injury, or destruction not necessary for the accomplishment of legitimate military purposes. It forms the basis of the prohibition of unnecessary suffering, the requirement of proportionality, and the immunity of civilians and the civilian population from being made the object of attack. The concept of chivalry is reflected in specific prohibitions, such as those against dishonourable or treacherous conduct, against misuse of enemy flags or flags of truce, etc, and acknowledges that opposing combatants were entitled to respect and honour. The law of armed conflict and the customary law of targeting is rooted in the principle that a

22 Mallison Sally V. and Mallison W. Thomas, Naval Targeting: Lawful Objects of Attack, *International Law Review*, Vol. 64, pp. 241-299.

23 UK Manual on the Law of Armed Conflict (2004), paragraph 2.2, where the reference to partial submission is intended to reflect the perhaps limited purpose of some conflicts.

distinction must be made throughout the conflict between those who may be lawfully attacked and those who must be respected and protected. The latter category includes civilians. No matter how pressing or dangerous the military circumstance is, only that kind of force which the law permits may be used.[24]

Military Objectives

Objects qualifying as military objectives are all warships, military aircraft, and other military equipment; which by their nature, location, purpose or use, effectively contribute to the enemy's war-fighting or war-sustaining capability and whose total or partial destruction or neutralisation would constitute a definite military advantage.[25] Therefore, the sinking of an enemy warship will always be following the law of naval warfare. They may be attacked as long as they are encountered outside neutral waters. Therefore, the sinking of the *General Belgrano*, during the 1982 Falklands/Malvinas conflict, was in accordance with the law of naval warfare although the *Belgrano* had been encountered outside the British Total Exclusion Zone.

According to the principle of customary international humanitarian law (IHL), parties to an armed conflict must always distinguish between the civilian population and combatants and between civilian objects and military objectives. To spare the civilians from hostilities and their effects, it is essential that the intended target of 'attack' must be a combatant or military objective.[26] Once a military objective is a target, under the rule of

24 Boothby William H., 2012, *The Law of Targeting*, Oxford: Oxford University Press, pp. 58-61.

25 The following activities render merchant vessels military objectives: (i) engaging in belligerent acts on behalf of the enemy, e.g., laying mines, minesweeping, engaging in visit and search or attacking other merchant vessels; (ii) acting as an auxiliary to an enemy's armed forces, e.g., carrying troops or replenishing warships; (iii) being incorporated into or assisting the enemy's intelligence gathering system, e.g., engaging in reconnaissance, early warning, surveillance, or command, control and communications missions; (iv) sailing under convoy of enemy warships or military aircraft; (v) refusing an order to stop or actively resisting visit, search or capture; being armed to an extent that they could inflict damage to a warship; this excludes light individual weapons for the defence of personnel, e.g., against pirates, and purely deflective systems such as chaff. Gill Terry D. and Fleck Dieter, 2015, *The Handbook of the International Law of Military Operations*, Oxford: Oxford University Press, p. 408.

26 Combatants are military objectives. Police officers are combatants if they are incorporated into the armed forces. Civilians, including police officers not incorporated into the armed forces, who unlawfully take a direct part in hostilities,

proportionality, the attack would be illegal if excessive collateral damage affecting civilians or civilian objects is expected.[27] Furthermore, while attacking a lawful target, precautionary measures to spare civilians must be taken.[28]

Targeting

The law of naval targeting is based upon three fundamental principles: (i) The right of belligerents to adopt means of injuring the enemy is not unlimited; (ii) It is prohibited to launch attacks against the civilian population as such; and (iii) Distinctions must be made between combatants and civilians, to the effect that the civilians be spared as much as possible. As discussed above, IHL requires that only militarily significant objectives be attacked, but it permits the use of sufficient mass to destroy those objectives. One of the important principles of war, the economy of force, requires that no more effort should be directed against a military objective than is necessary to accomplish it. In addition, the law of naval targeting provides that all reasonable precautions must be taken to ensure that only military objectives are targeted and that non-combatants and civilian objects are spared as much as possible from the effects of armed conflict.

---

lose their protection against attacks, as long as they directly participate. Everyone else who is not a combatant is a civilian benefiting from the protection provided for by the law on the conduct of hostilities. Military objectives, such as armament factories, may be attacked, and, subject to the principle of proportionality, the attack on a military objective does not become unlawful because of the risk that a civilian who works or is otherwise present in a military objective may be harmed by such an attack. There is therefore no military necessity that the armament worker or the weapons development scientist might be targeted individually, e.g., through aerial bombardment of the residential area where he lives or by enemy ground forces capturing his factory.

27 The principle of proportionality is often misapplied. For instance, in some cases the mere quantum of collateral damage and incidental injury causes critics to condemn a strike as disproportionate. However, the extent of harm and damage is relevant only in relation to the military advantage reasonably expected as the attack was launched. The standard is "excessive" (a comparative concept), not "extensive" (an absolute concept). Schmitt Michael N., Precision Attack and International Humanitarian Law, *International Review of the Red Cross*, Vol. 87, No. 859, 2005, pp. 445-466.

28 Sassoli Marco, Legitimate Targets of Attacks under International Humanitarian Law, Background Paper for the Informal High-Level Expert Meeting on the Reaffirmation and Development of International Humanitarian Law, Cambridge, January 27-29, 2003, Programme on Humanitarian Policy and Conflict Research at Harvard University.

Target Selection

The targets for naval attack include enemy warships and military aircraft, naval and military auxiliaries, naval and military bases ashore, warship construction and repair facilities, military depots and warehouses, petroleum and oil (POL) storage areas, docks, port facilities, harbours, bridges, airfields, military vehicles, armour, artillery, ammunition stores, troop concentrations and embarkation points, communication systems and other objects used to conduct or support military operations. The naval targets also include geographic targets, such as a mountain pass, and facilities that provide administrative and personnel support for military and naval operations such as barracks, communications and command and control facilities, headquarters buildings, and training areas.[29]

The economic targets for naval attack include enemy lines of communication, rail yards, bridges, industrial installations producing war-fighting products, and power generation plants. Economic targets which effectively support and sustain the enemy's war-fighting capability may also be attacked. While targeting, all reasonable precautions must be taken to ensure that only military objectives are targeted so that civilians and civilian objects are spared as much as possible from the ravages of war.[30] The intentional destruction of food, crops, livestock, drinking water and other objects indispensable to the survival of the civilian population, for the specific purpose of denying the civilian population their use, is prohibited.

The US Publication provides a list of "Category I No Strike Facilities", which are the most sensitive places protected by the law of armed conflict or IHL, other international and domestic laws, and the state policies.[31]

29 Para 8.1.1, *Annotated Supplement to the Commander's Handbook* (1997).

30 Article 52, paragraph 2, AP I.

31 The US publication "No-Strike and Collateral Damage Estimation Methodology" issued by the Chairman of the Joint Chief of Staff states that it is an inherent responsibility of all commanders, observers, air battle managers, weapons directors, attack controllers, weapons systems operators, intelligence analysts, and targeting personnel to: (a) Establish positive identification (PID) and to accurately locate targets consistent with current military objectives and mission specific ROE. The term "PID" is defined as follows: "The reasonable certainty that a functionally and geospatially defined object of attack is a legitimate military target in accordance with the laws of war and applicable ROE." (b) Identify potential collateral (i.e., No-strike) concerns in the vicinity of the valid military target prior to munitions release and target engagement (provide function and geospatial delimitations if able).(c) Apply the collateral damage estimation methodology (CDM) with due diligence within the framework of the operational imperatives of accomplishing mission objectives, force

These objects typically constitute the core of the No Strike List (NSL) and include:

- Diplomatic offices, foreign missions, and sovereign nonmilitary property of other nations within the area of responsibility.
- Religious, cultural, historical institutions, cemeteries, and structures.
- Intergovernmental organisations (e.g., United Nations) and Nongovernmental organisations (e.g., ICRC) property, equipment, and personnel.
- Medical facilities (both civilian and military).
- Public education facilities including nonmilitary schools, colleges, universities, child/day care centres, and institutes.
- Civilian refugee camps and concentrations.
- Prisoner of war camps and concentrations and government detention facilities/prisons.
- Facilities whose engagement may result in pollution that cannot be contained to include contamination of standing water, streams, and rivers.
- Dams or dikes whose engagement may result in the flooding of civilian areas.

Environment Protection

War is synonymous with environmental damage and human casualties. Warfare will always have an adverse impact on the environment; the extent will depend on the willingness of warring sides to conform to environmental regulations that may constrain their ability to achieve victory in the war. Although international environmental laws are not aimed at naval operations specifically, they require compliance that impacts, directly or indirectly, on our ability to train effectively.[32] A naval

---

protection, and collateral damage mitigation. The US Chairman of the Joint Chief of Staff publication, "No-Strike and Collateral Damage Estimation Methodology," CJCSI 3160.01A, October 12, 2012, pp. 122.

32 Wright William H., Naval Warfare and The Environment, International Law Studies, Vol. 69, 1996, pp. 35-41.

commander must ensure that methods or means of warfare are used with due regard to the protection and preservation of the natural environment. He has an obligation to avoid unnecessary damage to the environment. The destruction of the natural environment not necessitated by mission accomplishment and carried out wantonly is prohibited.[33]

Post Attack Actions

After each engagement, belligerents must, without delay, search for and collect the shipwrecked, wounded and sick, and recover the dead.[34] The crews of captured or destroyed enemy warships, military aircraft, and naval and military auxiliaries should be made POWs.

Actions not considered an "Attack"

In the context of naval warfare, the following actions are not considered as an attack:

(i) Declaring and establishing a blockade. However, a vessel that

33 Article 35 (paragraph 3), and 55 of AP I; The 1977 Convention on the Prohibition of Military or Any Other Hostile Use of Environmental Modification Techniques (ENMOD); The UN General Assembly Resolutions A/47/37 and A/49/50, adopted on November 25, 1992 and December 9, 1994, also call upon States to incorporate into their military manuals' guidance on the international law applicable to protection of the environment in time of armed conflict. The ICRC has compiled "Guidance for Military Manuals and Instructions on the Protection of the Environment in Times of Armed Conflict," which are annexed to UN document A/49/323 (1994). Paragraph 44 of the San Remo Manual provides: "Methods and means of warfare should be employed with due regard for the natural environment taking into account the relevant rules of international law. Damage to or destruction of the natural environment not justified by military necessity and carried out wantonly is prohibited."

34 Hague Convention (X) of 1907 for the Adaptation to Maritime Warfare of the Principles of the Geneva Convention requires belligerents to "take steps to look for the shipwrecked," after each engagement, "so far as military interests permit." This obligation is addressed more stringently in GC II (Geneva Convention of 1949 for the Amelioration of the Condition of Wounded, Sick and Shipwrecked Members of Armed Forces at Sea). Article 18 of GC II does not refer to military interests, and obligates Parties to act without delay: "After each engagement, Parties to the conflict shall, without delay, take all possible measures to search for and collect the shipwrecked, wounded and sick, to protect them against pillage and ill-treatment, to ensure their adequate care, and to search for the dead and prevent their being despoiled. Whenever circumstances permit, the Parties to the conflict shall conclude local arrangements for the removal of the wounded and sick by sea from a besieged or encircled area and for the passage of medical and religious personnel and equipment on their way to that area." Article 10, AP I enunciate a general obligation to respect and protect the shipwrecked.

breaches a blockade and resists enforcement measures by the blockading party renders itself liable to attack. Any such attack is governed by the rules set out in this chapter.

(ii) Declaring a maritime zone or implementing restrictions in the immediate vicinity of naval operations does not qualify as an attack. However, vessels that resist enforcement measures may render themselves liable to attack, which would be governed by the rules in this chapter.

(iii) Capture as booty of war or prize is a discrete act and does not constitute an attack. Vessels that resist capture may render themselves liable to attack. Similarly, Belligerent destruction of prizes or captured booty of war is also not considered an act of attack.

(iv) Visit, board, search, and seizure (VBSS) also do not constitute an attack, but where a vessel clearly resists such measures, it renders itself liable to attack.

(v) In the context of naval mine warfare, laying a minefield, either at sea or on land, never in itself constitutes an attack. An activation of these mines constitutes an attack. Laying of automatic contact mines to protect a particular location, or a minefield established for anti-access/area denial (A2/AD) purposes does not constitute an attack. It is regulated, however, by the rules set out in Hague Convention VIII. Laying a mine (whether tethered or not) that can identify a particular vessel is not an attack. However, it constitutes an attack at the point at which the mine is activated to detonate.

Immunity from An Attack

Certain classes of enemy vessels and aircraft are exempt under the law of naval warfare from capture, attack or destruction, provided they are innocently employed in their exempt category. These specially protected vessels and aircraft must not take part in the hostilities, must not hamper the movement of combatants, must submit to identification and inspection procedures, and may be ordered out of harm's way. The following classes of enemy vessels are exempt from attack:

- Hospital ships; small craft used for coastal rescue operations and other medical transports;[35]

- Vessels granted safe conduct by agreement between the belligerents, for instance carrying prisoners of war;

- Vessels engaged in transporting cultural property under special protection;

- Passenger vessels when engaged only in carrying civilian passengers;

- Vessels charged with religious, non-military scientific, or philanthropic missions, and vessels collecting scientific data of likely military applications are not protected;

- Small coastal fishing vessels and small boats engaged in local coastal trade, but they are subject to the regulations of a belligerent naval commander operating in the area and to inspection;

- Vessels designed or adapted exclusively for responding to pollution incidents in the marine environment;

- Vessels which have surrendered;

- Life rafts and lifeboats.

The exemption from attacks on the vessels listed above is based on the 1907 Hague Convention XI and customary international law as reflected in military manuals. Hospital ships remain to be protected against attack if they communicate via satellites, i.e., by using encryption. Although Article 34(2) of the Second Geneva Convention provides that 'hospital ships may not possess or use a secret code for their wireless or other means of communication', there is widespread agreement today that the prohibition of Article 34(2) GC II has become obsolete by derogation

35 Hospital ships remain to be protected against attack if they communicate via satellites, i.e., by using encryption. Although Article 34(2) of the Second Geneva Convention of 1949 provides that 'hospital ships may not possess or use a secret code for their wireless or other means of communication', there is widespread agreement today that the prohibition of Article 34(2) GC II has become obsolete by derogation through subsequent State practice. Technological requirements of modern communication have clearly rendered this provision of Geneva Convention outdated. The same holds true for the prohibition on arming hospital ships if and in so far as hospital ships are equipped with deflective means like chaff and flares. Gill Terry D. and Fleck Dieter, 2015, *The Handbook of the International Law of Military Operations*, Oxford: Oxford University Press, pp. 743, at p. 404.

through subsequent State practice. Technological requirements of modern communication have rendered this provision of the Geneva Convention outdated. The same holds for the prohibition on arming hospital ships if and in so far as hospital ships are equipped with deflective means like chaff and flares. The 2016 US Law of War Manual states, "In light of the requirement for encryption in modern communications systems (*e.g.*, satellite communications and video teleconference systems) and navigational technology (*e.g.*, global positioning systems) and the goal of ensuring that hospital ships can effectively fulfil their humanitarian mission, the US has employed hospital ships with the capability to conduct encrypted communications."[36] Hospital ships may not use encrypted communications for military purposes (*e.g.*, transmitting intelligence data) or in any way that is harmful to an adversary. Commissioners or neutral observers may be placed on board hospital ships to verify compliance with this rule.

Article 35 of the Second Geneva Convention lists five conditions that do not deprive hospital ships and sick-bays of warships of their special protection. These are: (i) The crews of ships or sick-bays are armed for the maintenance of order, for their defence or that of the sick and wounded; (ii) The presence on board of apparatus exclusively intended to facilitate navigation or communication; (iii) The discovery on board hospital ships or in sick-bays of portable arms and ammunition taken from the wounded, sick and shipwrecked and not yet handed to the proper service; (iv) The humanitarian activities of hospital ships and sick-bays of vessels or the crews extend to the care of wounded, sick or shipwrecked civilians; and (v) The transport of equipment and personnel intended exclusively for medical duties, over and above the normal requirements.

Naval Bombardment of Land Targets

The general limitations on bombardment are derived from the basic principle of humanity. It states that the wanton destruction of cities, towns, or villages, or any devastation not justified by military necessity, is prohibited. The term bombardment as used herein includes both aerial and naval bombardment. In 1895 the Institute of International Law appointed a committee to consider proposed rules of bombardment for naval warfare, similar to those applicable to land warfare. However, participating states declined to accept the proposal. The Hague Convention IX (1907)

36 The Department of Defence Law of War Manual (updated December 2016), United States of America, para 7.12.2.7.

Respecting Bombardment by Naval Forces[37] establishes the general rules of naval bombardment of land targets. These rules were further developed by customary practice in World Wars I and II, Vietnam, the Falkland Conflict and the Persian Gulf conflict. Underlying these rules are the broad principles of IHL that belligerents are forbidden to make non-combatants the target of direct attack, that superfluous injury and unnecessary suffering are to be avoided, and that wanton destruction of property is prohibited.

Article 1 of the Convention states that the bombardment by naval forces of undefended ports, towns, villages, dwellings, or buildings is forbidden. A place cannot be bombarded solely because automatic submarine contact mines are anchored off the harbour. Article 2 further clarifies that military works, military or naval establishments, depots of arms or war material, workshops or plants which could be utilised for the needs of the hostile fleet or army, and the ships of war in the harbour, are not, however, included in this prohibition. The commander of a naval force may destroy them with artillery, after a summons followed by a reasonable time of waiting, if all other means are impossible, and when the local authorities have not themselves destroyed them within the time fixed. The military commander incurs no responsibility for any unavoidable damage which may be caused by a bombardment under such circumstances.

Article 3 states that after due notice has been given, the bombardment of undefended ports, towns, villages, dwellings, or buildings may be commenced, if the local authorities, after a formal summons has been made to them, decline to comply with requisitions for provisions or supplies necessary for the immediate use of the naval force before the place in question. These requisitions shall be in proportion to the resources of the place. They shall only be demanded in the name of the commander of the said naval force, and they shall, as far as possible, be paid for in cash; if not, they shall be evidenced by receipts. Under Article 4 it is also prohibited to bombard undefended ports, towns, villages, dwellings, or buildings on account of failure to pay money contributions.

In any naval bombardment, Article 5 requires that all the necessary measures must be taken by the commander to spare as far as possible sacred edifices, buildings used for artistic, scientific, or charitable purposes, historic monuments, hospitals, and places where the sick or wounded are collected, on the understanding that they are not used at the same time for

37 Convention (IX) concerning Bombardment by Naval Forces in Time of War, The Hague, October 18, 1907. The states who are party to 1977 AP I, the 1907 rules have been incorporated in Article 49(3) of 1977 AP I.

military purposes. A duty was placed on the inhabitants to indicate such monuments, edifices, or places by visible signs and if the military situation permits, the commander of the attacking naval force, before commencing the bombardment, is required to do his utmost to warn the authorities. The operative provisions of the Convention concluded with a prohibition of pillage, even where the town or place is taken by storm.[38] To give effect to the concepts of humanitarian law, the following general rules governing bombardment must be observed.

- A military objective within a city, town or village may, however, be bombarded if required for the submission of the enemy with the minimum expenditure of time, life and physical resources. However, incidental injury to civilians or collateral damage to civilian objects must not be excessive in light of the military advantage anticipated by the attack.

- Medical establishments and units (both mobile and fixed), medical vehicles, and medical equipment and stores may not be deliberately bombarded. Belligerents are required to ensure that such medical facilities are, as far as possible, situated in such a manner that attacks against military targets in the vicinity do not imperil their safety. A distinctive medical emblem, a Red Cross, Red Crescent or Red Crystal is to be displayed on medical establishments and units in order to identify them as entitled to protected status. If medical facilities are used for military purposes inconsistent with their humanitarian mission, the facilities become subject to attack. These provisions have now been covered under the universally ratified Second Geneva Convention of 1949.

- Bombardment for the sole purpose of terrorising the civilian population is prohibited.

- Belligerents are forbidden to bombard a city or town that is undefended and that is open to immediate entry by their own or allied forces.

- An agreed demilitarised zone is also exempt from bombardment.

38 Articles 6 and 7, Convention (IX) concerning Bombardment by Naval Forces in Time of War.

Attack on Dual-Use Targets

A dual-use target has both civilian and military functions, such as an airfield, port, electric power grid, oil-refining facilities, railways, bridges, and radio and TV broadcasting facilities, and public utilities providing support to both the civilian population and the military effort. The term "dual-use" target does not appear in the 1949 Geneva Conventions and their Additional Protocols. The dual-use targets serve the needs of both the civilian community and the armed forces. In industrialised, urbanised states in which such potential military objects are intermingled, it would be difficult to neutralise the military effectiveness of those targets without simultaneously harming the civilian population. For instance, the destruction of the electric power grid will degrade the enemy's communication facilities, however, it will also cut off the power supply to civil hospitals, domestic water supply systems and sewage plants. [39]

On May 15, 2021, the Israel Defence Force (IDF) attacked the Al-Jalaa Tower, a 12-story building in the Gaza Strip. The building, which was destroyed, housed the Associated Press and Al Jazeera offices, as well as civilian apartments.[40] According to IDF, the building "contained military assets of the Hamas terror organisation," which used the building for unlawful human shielding.[41] Israel's Ambassador to the US later told Associated Press executives that Hamas was using the building to develop a means of disrupting Israel's Iron Dome system. Israel gave occupants a one-hour

39 Solis D. Gary, 2016, *The Law of Armed Conflict: International Humanitarian Law in War*, Cambridge: Cambridge University Press, pp. 521-524.

40 The building had 11 floors, around 60 residential apartments, and offices for doctors, lawyers, and journalists including Al Jazeera and the Associated Press. Residents grabbed what belongings they could carry and ran down the stairs. Children and the elderly took turns using the single working elevator. An hour later, the IDF levelled the building and crushed everything inside.

41 Human shields are civilian or noncombatant personnel placed in or around a valid military target to hinder attack of that target. In some instances, human shields are willing accomplices who support the belligerent nation. In this case, they lose their protected status. In other instances, the belligerent nation may either forcibly place (involuntary) or deceptively encourage (unwitting) civilians or noncombatants to be present at valid military targets, and these personnel are considered protected persons. The US Chairman of the Joint Chief of Staff publication, "No-Strike and Collateral Damage Estimation Methodology," CJCSI 3160.01A, October 12, 2012, pp. 122, page B-8.

warning by various means and the building was evacuated before being struck.[42]

During the 1991 Operation Desert Strom, power grids were perceived as military targets. During Op Allied Force, the 1999 NATO bombing of Serbian targets, including some in the Yugoslav capital, the Serbian state television and radio station, RTS, in Belgrade was bombed. There is universal consensus that if a civilian building is being used to effectively promote or support military operations, it becomes a military objective; because targeting the building will result in a definite military advantage for the attacker. The 1954 Convention for the Protection of Cultural Property in the Event of Armed Conflict refers to an aerodrome, port and railway station as military objectives.[43]

The Danish Military Manual (2020) provides clarification in this regard. It states, "As far as dual-use objects are concerned, the entire object constitutes a military objective. Under international law, this means that damage to the dual-use object is not regarded as collateral either in whole or in part if the object is effectively indivisible. As a rule, the non-military 'share' of the object should not be taken into consideration in the proportionality assessment."[44] The US Department of Defence's Law of War Manual (2016) states, "If an object is a military objective, it is not a civilian object and may be made the object of attack."[45] To resolve this issue, the ICRC suggests that "while the dual use object is a military objective, the impact of the attack on the civilian part or component of the must also be taken into consideration in the assessment of proportionality."

The Indian armed forces are bound by the Hague and Geneva Conventions but not by the 1977 AP I. While targeting dual-use military objectives, weapons systems which can avoid the destruction of the objective may be used. Proportionality prohibits causing excessive damage to civilian objects and civilians when attacking a military objective. They must also keep in mind that proportionality cannot be assessed before every single shot fired, or every missile launched. To further the goals of the principle

42 Schmitt Michael N., Targeting Dual-Use Structure: An Alternative Interpretation, June 28, 2021, Lieber Institute, West Point.

43 The Convention for the Protection of Cultural Property in the Event of Armed Conflict, 1954, Article 8.1(a).

44 Military Manual on International Law Relevant to Danish Armed Forces in International Operations, Danish Ministry of Defence, 2020, Chapter 8, p. 310.

45 The US Department of Defence's Law of War Manual (edition 2016) para 5.6.1.2.

of proportionality, commanders should look at the big picture to assess alternative attacks that might cause less harm to civilians.[46]

Establishing Special Zones

Special zones may be established for:

(i) Defending objects and installations of high military value;

(ii) Containing the geographic area of military operations;

(iii) Subjecting civil navigation and/or aviation to restrictions or contraband control; or

(iv) Safeguarding protected persons, works and installations containing dangerous forces, objects and installations for the medical treatment of wounded and sick civilians or combatants, or objects protected under the law of armed conflict such as cultural property.

An 'exclusion zone' is a three-dimensional area/space beyond the territorial sovereignty of any state. A belligerent, in an exclusion zone, can claim to be relieved from certain rules of the law of international armed conflict or where that belligerent party purports to be entitled to restrict the freedom of navigation (or aviation) of other states. Since the 1990s, exclusion zones have become a reality and they have been recognised as a lawful method of warfare in military manuals. Notice of the existence of these war zones must give the extent, location, duration, and associated risks. The right to fire upon any aircraft disregarding a general prohibition of entry into such a zone must be based on military necessity.[47] 'Exclusion zones' and 'no-fly zones' must be clearly distinguished from blockades. Zones must

46 Regarding the practice of states, many countries have made declarations upon ratification of 1977 AP I that the military advantage means, "the advantage anticipated from the military attack *considered as a whole* and not only from isolated or particular parts of that attack." These states include Canada, Cote d'Ivoire, France, Germany, Italy, New Zealand, Nigeria, Spain, and the United Kingdom. The government of Belgium declared that military advantage would be "from an attack considered in its totality." This is also the position of the United States and Israel, which are not parties to the protocol but do apply many of its provisions, because they view them as part of customary international law. Cohen Amichai and David Zlotogorski, 2021, *Proportionality in International Humanitarian Law: Consequences, Precautions, and Procedures*, Oxford: Oxford University Press, p. 262, at pp. 66-72.

47 The UK Manual on Law of Armed Conflict, 2004, paras 12.58, 13.77; German Law of Armed Conflict Manual, Joint Service Regulation (ZDv) 15/2, Federal Ministry of Defence, May 1, 2013, para 1058.

be distinguished from the rights enjoyed by belligerents near (naval) operations and for force protection. A further purpose an exclusion zone may lawfully serve is the safeguarding of persons and objects protected under the law of international armed conflict. The opposing belligerent party is not obliged to refrain from conducting hostilities within the zone as long as the rules of the law of international armed conflict on protected persons and objects are observed.[48]

48 Gill Terry D. and Fleck Dieter, 2015, *The Handbook of the International Law of Military Operations*, Oxford: Oxford University Press, pp. 414-415.

Section 2

Maritime Operations and Legality

III

Maritime Blockade

During an armed conflict, a belligerent power can pursue several alternative military and naval strategies in that country's efforts to defeat its enemies. For instance, economic warfare, by weakening the enemy's ability to pursue military action, can be a substitute for direct combat. Such an economic strategy can sever the trading links between the enemy and his allies to reduce the level of military and civilian goods that are available to support his military ventures.

A blockade is a belligerent operation to prevent vessels of all nations, enemy as well as neutral, from entering or exiting specified ports or coastal areas belonging to, occupied by, or under the control of an enemy nation. Historically, the naval blockade has been the most common form of economic warfare. In simple terms, a naval blockade can be viewed as an attempt by one belligerent, through the interception by sea of the approaches to the coasts or ports of an enemy, to cut off all his overseas communications via maritime route. The general aim is to reduce the enemy's ability to effectively carry out military operations. Although most blockades are deployed by belligerent powers in wartime, blockades have been used to deter war by weakening a potential enemy before an official declaration of war.[1] The purpose of a naval blockade is to help achieve the overall objective of the use of armed force, i.e., to get the enemy to agree to terms favourable to you through undermining the enemy's war effort by interdicting in- and outgoing maritime traffic.[2]

The naval blockade is a classic strategy for gaining sea control or imposing sea denial and has been used as a military tactic throughout history. During

1 Davis Lance E. and Engerman Stanley L., 2006, *Naval Blockades in Peace and War: An Economic History Since 1750*, Cambridge: Cambridge University Press, p. 453.

2 Frostad Magne, Naval Blockade, *Arctic Review on Law and Politics*, Vol. 9, 2018, p. 195.

the eighteenth century, blockade became a routine practice in a European conflict. But the difficulty of blockading long coastlines soon gave rise to the 'paper blockade', in which a nation might declare a blockade, but lack the naval force to effectively maintain it.[3] During the US Civil War, the Union forces blockaded southern ports to prevent the export of cotton to Britain and other countries and to prevent the import of food and supplies.

Blockades have continued to be used in several contemporary international armed conflicts. For example, Egypt's blockades against Israeli shipping in the late 1940s and early 1950s, during the Suez Canal Crisis of 1956 and in 1967 just before the Six-Day War. The US blockade of Cuba of October 1962 (The Cuban missile crisis) to prevent Russian freighters from bringing missile components to Cuba, and blockades during the Vietnam War.[4] In 1967, Egypt closed the Gulf of Aqaba and the Straits of Tiran to Israeli shipping. In March 1965, China conducted a ballistic missile test close to Taiwan's major ports; the missile launches were variously described in the media and by Western experts as a "de facto," "partial," "temporary," or "cold" blockade.[5] Between 1966 and 1975, the British Royal Navy conducted one of the more unusual blockades of modern history – a maritime-intercept operation that became known as the "Beira patrol."[6] The Indo-Pakistan

3 The early Dutch blockades of England (1662) and France (1672–1673) and the Dutch–English blockade (1689) were regarded as paper blockades. Kraska James, Rule Selection in the Case of Israel's Naval Blockade of Gaza: Law of Naval Warfare or Law of the Sea, *Yearbook of International Humanitarian Law*, Vol. 13, 2010, pp. 367–395, 380.

4 The US applied something resembling a blockade to North Vietnam in May 1972 through the use of mines, although the term blockade was not officially used. Jones Thomas David, *The International Law of Maritime Blockade: A Measure of Naval Economic Interdiction, Howard Law Journal*, Vol. 26, 1983, pp. 759-780.

5 The use of ballistic missiles as a means to enforce a blockade, even a partial or temporary one, would seem to be isolated to the Taiwan situation. Although not specifically referring to a blockade scenario, a Pentagon analyst has noted that "the Taiwan Strait case may be unique in that it is the first theatre in which highly accurate *conventional* ballistic missiles dominate the strategic landscape." Rahman Chris, "Ballistic Missiles in China's Anti-Taiwan Blockade Strategy," in Elleman Bruce A. and Paine S.C.M. (ed.), *Naval Blockades and Seapower: Strategies and Counter-Strategies, 1805–2005*, London: Routledge, pp. 215-223.

6 The Royal Navy and Royal Air Force monitored shipping in the Mozambique Channel in an attempt to cut oil supplies from reaching landlocked Southern Rhodesia (today Zimbabwe) via the port of Beira, in the Portuguese colony of Mozambique. Although the blockade was successful, Britain's overall oil embargo against Rhodesia failed. London could not extend maritime interception operations to other ports in Mozambique or elsewhere, yet it refused to abandon a mission that was increasingly unpopular within the Navy. Only when Mozambique gained independence from

War (1971) lasted a mere thirteen days but included submarine attacks on surface warships and an Indian blockade of the East Pakistan/Bangladesh coast in the Bay of Bengal.[7] More recent blockades include UN Security Council-approved 'military intercept' operations against Iraq (1999) and Yugoslavia (1991–1992), the Israeli blockade of 2010, the Saudi-Arabia-led coalition's blockade of Yemen (2015), and Russia's blockade of the Sea of Azov (2022).

Purpose and Types

According to the Indian Maritime Doctrine, the primary purpose of a blockade is to deny the enemy reinforcements, re-supply and maritime trade, thus degrading his war-waging capability. Blockades can also be used to enforce sanctions. A blockading force has the right to seize as prize any merchant ship – be it enemy or neutral – that attempts to run the blockade either inwards or outwards. As an additional benefit, blockade may be used for military containment by coercing enemy forces to remain behind the blockading line, thus ceding sea control and the use of the sea to the blockading navy. To be recognised under international law, a blockade must have been declared and notified to all concerned. It should also be effective and applied impartially to ships of all nations. A blockade must not bar access to or departure from neutral ports. Although neutral warships do not enjoy any right of access to blockaded areas, the belligerent imposing blockade may authorise their entry and exit. Such special authorisation may be made subject to conditions deemed necessary and expedient by the blockading force.[8]

The US Law of War Manual defines blockade as an operation by a belligerent State to prevent vessels and/or aircraft of all States, enemy as well as neutral, from entering or exiting specified ports, airfields, or coastal areas

---

Portugal in 1975, and could credibly assure the UN that no oil would cross its territory to Rhodesia, did the Beira patrol come to an end. Mobley Richard A., "The Beira Patrol: Britain's Broken Blockades Against Rhodesia," in Elleman Bruce A. and Paine S.C.M. (ed.), *Naval Blockades and Seapower: Strategies and Counter-Strategies, 1805–2005*, London: Routledge, pp. 181-188.

7 James Goldrick, No Easy Answers: The Development of the Navies of India, Bangladesh, Pakistan and Sri Lanka 1945–1996, Papers in Australian Maritime Affairs No. 2, Royal Australian Navy Maritime Studies Programme, Lancer Publishers, New Delhi, 1997, pp. 68–103; Samant MNR and Unnithan Sandeep, 2019, *Operation X: The Untold Story of India's Covert War in East Pakistan,* HarperCollins Publishers, India, p. 272.

8 Indian Maritime Doctrine, Indian Navy Naval Strategic Publication 1.1, Integrated Headquarters, Ministry of Defence (Navy) 2009, pp. 85-86.

belonging to, occupied by, or under the control of an enemy belligerent State. The purpose of a blockade is to deprive the adversary of supplies needed to conduct hostilities. It enables the blockading State to control traffic in the blockaded area. A blockade also enables the blockading State to take measures on the high seas to deny supplies to a blockaded area. For example, a blockading State has the right to visit and search vessels on the high seas to enforce its blockade.[9]

Blockade types include close and distant (in terms of the distance of the blockade perimeter from its focus), near and far (in terms of the distance of the theatre from the blockading country); partial and total (in terms of the blockade's porosity); and paper, pacific, and belligerent (in terms of the level of coercion). In addition, blockades can be executed unilaterally or in combination with a coalition, and they can be broken by blockade runners or by creating alternate landlines of communication or air routes.[10]

Legal Framework

Naval blockades in earlier times were largely aimed at the economy of the enemy, today they are often an integral part of military operations directed against the enemy's military assets. The traditional rules of the blockade are customary, having derived their definitive form through the practice of maritime powers during the nineteenth century. The rules reflect a balance between the right of a belligerent possessing effective command of the sea to close enemy ports and coastlines to international commerce, and the right of neutral nations to carry out neutral commerce with the least possible interference from belligerent forces. The blockade is a method of warfare to which the general principles of naval warfare apply.

State practices including Un-authorised blockades, have contributed to establishing the current principles governing naval blockades. According to the UN Charter, only the Security Council has the power to decide on sanctions, embargoes and blockades. Article 41 of the Charter mostly covers sanctions and embargoes. Military intervention is addressed by Article 42, which extends and clarifies the capabilities of the Security Council in these matters. "Should the Security Council consider that measures provided for in Article 41 would be inadequate or have proved to be inadequate, it may take such action by air, sea, or land forces as may

9 The US Department of Defence, Law of War Manual (edition 2016), p. 903.

10 Elleman Bruce A. and Paine S.C.M., "Conclusion: Naval Blockades and the Future of Seapower," in Elleman Bruce A. and Paine S.C.M. (ed.), *Naval Blockades and Seapower: Strategies and Counter-Strategies, 1805–2005*, London: Routledge, pp. 250-266.

be necessary to maintain or restore international peace and security. Such action may include demonstrations, blockade, and other operations by air, sea, or land forces of Members of the United Nations."

The Israeli-*Gaza Flotilla* incident raised many questions about international law and generated different views as to its lawfulness as reflected by two UN Reports and writings of jurists on the issue.[11] As reported, on May 31, 2010, Israeli military forces interdicted six passenger vessels carrying a total of 600 civilian activists and 10,000 tons of humanitarian assistance to the Gaza Strip, which was under both a naval and land blockade imposed by Israel. The blockade, referred to as the "*Gaza Flotilla* incident", was enforced by the Israeli Defence Force (IDF) in the high seas of the eastern Mediterranean Sea some 72 nautical miles from the nearest coast, and 64 nautical miles from the blockade zone declared by Israel. All six vessels were diverted to the Israeli port of Ashdod where 600 passengers were detained. Nine passengers lost their lives and many more other passengers were injured. Israeli justified the military interception on the high seas and use of force based on the customary international law of blockade.[12]

Five requirements had to be met before a naval blockade could exist under international law: (i) The blockade had to be established by one of

11 In response to the diplomatic crisis created by the incident, the UN Secretary stablished a UN Panel of Inquiry chaired by Sir Geoffrey Palmer. Parallel to the UN Panel of Inquiry the UN Human Rights Council conducted its own fact-finding mission pursuant to UNGA resolution 14/1 of 2 June 2010. The two reports arrived at different conclusions concerning the lawfulness of the naval blockade but agreed as to the unlawful enforcement by Israeli forces on the high seas. Also see: Douglas Guilfoyle, The Mavi Marmara Incident and Blockade in Armed Conflict, *British Yearbook of International Law*, Vol. 81, 2011, pp. 171–223; George Bisharat, Carey James and Rose Mishaan, Freedom Thwarted: Israel's Illegal Attack on the Gaza Flotilla, *Berkeley Journal of Middle Eastern and Islamic Law*, Vol. 4, 2011, pp. 79–110; Russell Buchan, The Palmer Report and the Legality of Israel's Naval Blockade of Gaza, *International and Comparative Law Quarterly*, Vol. 61, 2012, pp. 264–273; *Kraska* James and Raul Pedroza, 2013, *International Maritime Security Law*, Leiden: Martinus Nijhoff, pp. 895–899; and Azzali Pietro, The Naval Blockade of the Gaza Strip: A Law of the Sea Perspective, Master Thesis, The Arctic University of Norway, 2015, p. 48.

12 On May 31, 2010, the Turkish ship *Mavi Marmara* attempted to breach the Israel naval blockade of the coast of Gaza. Six of the seven ships of the flotilla were intercepted and escorted to port without a violent incident. The *Mavi Marmara* was boarded by Israel military personnel and a violent clash ensued between Israel military personnel and operatives of the IHH, a radical Islamic group aboard the ship, resulting in the death of eight IHH persons, one Turkish national, and several Israel military casualties. It is believed that the sponsors of the *Mavi Marmara* had two objectives: one, to deliver humanitarian aid to Gaza; and two, to provoke a confrontation with Israel in the hope that they would overreact.

the parties, (ii) It must be proclaimed by such a party, (iii) Blockade must be effective, (iv) It must be applied impartially, and (v) Blockade must not hinder travel to and from any points of a neutral coastline. If these requirements were met, the blockading power was entitled to visit and search, capture, and in extreme situations destroy, vessels seeking to breach the blockade.[13] According to London Declaration (1909), to be valid under the customary rules of international law, a blockade must conform to the following criteria:[14]

- A blockade must be established by the government of the belligerent nation. This is usually accomplished by a declaration of the belligerent government or by the commander of the blockading force acting on behalf of his government.

- The declaration should include, as a minimum, the date the blockade is to begin, its geographical limits, and the grace period granted to neutral vessels and aircraft to leave the area to be blockaded.

- It is customary for the belligerent nation establishing the blockade to notify all affected nations of its imposition.

- In order to be valid, a blockade must be effective. To be effective, it must be maintained by a surface, air or subsurface force or other mechanism that is sufficient to render ingress or egress of the blockaded area dangerous.[15]

- A blockade must be applied impartially to the vessels and aircraft of all nations. Discrimination by the blockading belligerent in favour of or against the vessels and aircraft of particular nations, including those of its own or those of an allied nation, renders the blockade legally invalid.

13 Frostad Magne, Naval Blockade, *Arctic Review on Law and Politics*, Vol. 9, 2018, pp. 195–225.

14 Articles 4, 8, 9 and 12, London Declaration 1909.

15 This requirement of effectiveness is intended to prevent "paper" blockades. The requirement of effectiveness means that the blockade must be maintained by forces that are sufficient to render ingress or egress of the blockaded area dangerous. The requirement of effectiveness does not preclude temporary absence of the blockading force, if such absence is due to stress of weather or to some other reason connected with the blockade (*e.g.*, pursuit of a blockade runner). The forces that are necessary to make a blockade effective depend on the specific military circumstances. The blockade may be maintained by forces that are some distance from the shore.

- A blockade must not bar access to or departure from neutral ports and coasts. Neutral nations retain the right to engage in neutral commerce that does not involve trade or communications originating in or destined for the blockaded area.

- Although neutral warships and military aircraft enjoy no positive right of access to blockaded areas, the belligerent imposing the blockade may authorise their entry and exit. Such special authorisation may be made subject to such conditions as the blockading force considers necessary and expedient.

- Neutral vessels in distress should be authorised entry into a blockaded area, and subsequently authorised to depart, under conditions prescribed by the officer in command of the blockading force.[16]

- Neutral vessels engaged in the carriage of relief supplies for the civilian population and the sick and wounded should be authorised to pass through the blockade cordon.[17]

- A blockade may not be used for the purpose of starving the civilian population, and the expected incidental harm to the civilian population may not be excessive in relation to the expected military advantage to be gained from employing the blockade.[18]

The intentional destruction of an economy through blockade can cause starvation, suffering and death amongst the civilian population that relies on it. Several examples in history show that prolonged blockades can have disastrous consequences for the civilian population. Article 51 of AP I is one of the most important articles in the Protocol. It explicitly confirms the customary rule that innocent civilians must be kept outside hostilities as far as possible and enjoy general protection against danger arising from hostilities. Article 51 establishes bases for the prohibitions and precautions

16 A vessel sailing ignorantly (*i.e.*, with neither presumptive nor actual knowledge) to a blockaded port is not liable to capture, although it may be turned away from the blockaded area. *Yeaton v. Fry*, 9 US 335-343 (1809).

17 Article 70(2), the 1977 AP I.

18 Starvation of civilians as a method of warfare is prohibited under Article 54 of the 1977 AP I.

that protect civilians and civilian objects from the effects of military operations.[19]

The US Commander's Handbook on the Law of Naval Operations (2022) [20] states that to be valid, a blockade must conform to the criteria in the following:

A. **Establishment**: A blockade must be established by the government of the belligerent State. This is accomplished by a declaration of the belligerent government or by the commander of the blockading force acting on behalf of the belligerent government. The declaration should include, at a minimum, the date the blockade is to begin, its geographic limits, and the grace period granting neutral vessels and aircraft to leave the area to be blockaded. Although it is the customary practice of States when declaring a blockage to specify a period during which neutral vessels and aircraft may leave the blockaded area, there is no uniformity with respect to the length of the grace period. A belligerent declaring a blockade is free to fix as long a grace period as it considers reasonable under the circumstances.

B. **Notification**: It is customary for the belligerent State establishing the blockade to notify all affected States of its imposition. Because knowledge of the existence of a blockade is an essential element of the offences of breach and attempted breach of blockade, neutral vessels and aircraft are always entitled to notification. The commander of the blockading forces will notify local authorities in the blockaded area. The form of the notification is not material, so long as it is effective.

C. **Effectiveness**: To be valid, a blockade must be effective. It must be maintained by a surface, air, or subsurface force or other legitimate methods and means of warfare that are sufficient to render ingress

19 Drew Phillip Jeffrey, An Analysis of the Legality of Maritime Blockade in the Context of Twenty-First Century Humanitarian Law, Thesis for Master of Law, Australian National University, March 2012, p. 123.

20 The US has recently released The Commander's Handbook on the Law of Naval Operations, March 2022. This is a tri-service publication applicable to the US Navy, Marine Corps and Coast Guard, and provides an overview of the legal rules governing naval operations in both peacetime and during armed conflict. Written for the war-fighter, it is intended for use by operational commanders and supporting staff elements at all levels of command. The publication also harmonizes with the Department of Defence, Law of War Manual (2016).

or egress of the blockaded area dangerous. The requirement of effectiveness does not preclude the temporary absence of the blockading force if such absence is due to the stress of weather or to some other reason connected with the blockade (e.g., the pursuit of a blockade runner). Effectiveness does not require every possible avenue of approach to the blockaded area to be covered. The forces necessary to make a blockade effective depend on the specific military circumstances. The blockade may be maintained by forces that are some distance from the shore.

D. **Impartiality**: A blockade must be applied impartially to the vessels and aircraft of all States. Discrimination by the blockading belligerent in favour of or against the vessels and aircraft of particular States, including those of its own or those of an allied State, renders the blockade legally invalid.

E. **Limitations**: A blockade must not bar access to or departure from neutral ports and coasts. The neutral States retain the right to engage in neutral commerce that does not involve trade or communications originating in or destined for the blockaded area. This means the blockade must not prevent trade and communication to or from neutral ports or coasts, provided such trade and communications are neither destined to nor originates from the blockaded area. A blockade is prohibited if the sole purpose is to starve the civilian population or deny it other objects essential for its survival.

It is widely accepted that a blockade, to be legally established, requires notification and enforcement effectively and impartially. The purpose of a blockade is to stop all ingress and egress of vessels of all States from an enemy coast or port. The legal issue is that once a blockade is legally established, it creates belligerent rights against other users of the sea, such as the seizure and capture of vessels irrespective of their flag. Also, vessels attempting to breach a blockade become liable to attack, after prior warning, by the blockading force.

Naval blockades are never conducted in a political vacuum but are a means to contribute to the achievement of national goals. A blockade must be established by proper legal authority. The Security Council has also expressly authorised blockade as self-defence under Chapter VII of the UN Charter. It is customary for the belligerent State establishing the blockade to notify all affected States of its imposition. The commander of the blockading forces usually notifies local authorities in the blockaded area. Notification should include, as a minimum, the date the blockade is to begin, its geographic limits, and the grace period granted to neutral vessels and aircraft to leave the area to be blockaded. The form of the notification is not material so long as it is effective, and a variety of methods may be used. The cessation, temporary lifting, re-establishment, extension, or other alteration of a blockade must be declared and notified.[21] A blockade may be enforced and maintained by a combination of legitimate methods and means of warfare provided this combination does not result in acts inconsistent with the rules of laws of war.

The San Remo Manual

The current legal framework for naval warfare rests upon rules of customary international law as reflected in the San Remo Manual, a non-binding document prepared by international law experts.[22] According to Manual (Articles 93 to 104), a blockade shall be declared and notified to all belligerents and neutral States. The declaration shall specify the commencement, duration, location, and extent of the blockade and the period within which vessels of neutral States may leave the blockaded coastline. A blockade must be effective, and the question of whether a blockade is effective is a question of fact. The force maintaining the blockade may be stationed at a distance determined by military requirements. A blockade may be enforced and maintained by a combination of legitimate methods and means of warfare provided this combination does not result in acts inconsistent with the rules of international laws of war. Merchant vessels believed on reasonable grounds to be breaching a blockade may be captured. Merchant vessels which, after prior warning, clearly resist capture

21 The Joint Service Manual of the Law of Armed Conflict, JSP 383, UK, Ministry of Defence, 2004, Para 13.73.

22 The current international framework for naval warfare at sea is found principally in the 1994 San Remo Manual on International Law Applicable to Armed Conflict at Sea, which was the outcome of a series of expert meetings conducted between 1988–1994 aimed at developing an instrument to both modernize the law of armed conflict at sea and clarify the existing state of customary law, especially on controversial issues such as exclusionary zones, or blockades. The Manual is one of the few comprehensive international instruments drafted in the twentieth century that guide determinations of legality regarding naval warfare. Although it is a legally recognized document, it represents a codification of customary international law and therefore is not fully binding. Biggs Adam, Xu Dan, Roaf Joshua, and Olson Tatana, Theories of Naval Blockades and Their Application in the Twenty-First Century, *Naval War College Review*, Vol. 74, No. 1, 2021, pp.2-31.

may be attacked.[23] A blockade must not bar access to the ports and coasts of neutral States. A blockade must be applied impartially to the vessels of all States. The cessation, temporary lifting, re-establishment, extension or other alteration of a blockade must be declared and notified.

According to San Remo Manual, the declaration or establishment of a blockade is prohibited if: (a) it has the sole purpose of starving the civilian population or denying it other objects essential for its survival; or (b) the damage to the civilian population is, or may be expected to be, excessive concerning the concrete and direct military advantage anticipated from the blockade. If the civilian population of the blockaded territory is inadequately provided with food and other objects essential for its survival, the blockading party must provide for free passage of such foodstuffs and other essential supplies, subject to (a) the right to prescribe the technical arrangements, including search, under which such passage is permitted; and (b) the condition that the distribution of such supplies shall be made under the local supervision of a humanitarian organisation which offers guarantees of impartiality, such as the International Committee of the Red Cross (ICRC). The blockading belligerent shall allow the passage of medical supplies for the civilian population or the wounded and sick members of armed forces, subject to the right to prescribe technical arrangements, including search, under which such passage is permitted. According to Dannenbaum (2021), restrictions provided in the San Remo framework are more demanding than existing IHL, including that codified in the 1977 AP I.[24]

Summation

The naval blockade continues to be a relevant part of modern naval strategy. A blockade is a useful means to regulate the competing interests of belligerents and neutrals in more limited armed conflict. According to Vego (2011), the successful conduct of naval warfare depends on one's ability to obtain and maintain or deny control of a part of the maritime

23 Article 67 of the Manual states that merchant vessels flying the flag of neutral States may be attacked if they are believed on reasonable grounds to be carrying contraband or breaching a blockade, and after prior warning they intentionally and clearly refuse to stop, or intentionally and clearly resist visit, search or capture.

24 Dannenbaum Tom, Encirclement, Deprivation, and Humanity: Revising the San Remo Manual Provisions on Blockade, *International Law Studies*, Vol. 97, 2021, pp. 307-394.

theatre.[25] Technological advancements in weapon systems, platforms, and communications, however, raise questions about the continuing relevance of blockade strategies and tactics that were developed during previous eras of naval warfare. It must be remembered that no blockade in history has been 100 per cent effective in preventing "contraband" from entering a blockaded state.

Blockades have been used primarily as wartime measures to reduce the military power of foes, and they have been employed by both sides of the conflict to seek an advantage. Given changes in the technology of warfare, the nature of the blockades has changed over time.[26] The Technology has enhanced the capabilities of naval forces to conduct reconnaissance and identification over wide areas of the ocean and to detect the presence of some contrabands that were previously undetectable. Modern technology like high-altitude reconnaissance drones, satellite communication and underwater fully autonomous weapons have changed the shape of blockades. The weapons for use in maritime environments have become longer in range, stealthier (which makes them more difficult to counter), and more accurate. Air-to-surface weapons have achieved high precision owing to satellite guidance against fixed targets and terminal homing against moving ones.[27] The blockading countries have moved away from underwater mines and shifted more toward air power. As a result, invasion of territory has become less common, while the threat of aerial attack is more common.

25 Milan Vego, Introduction to Naval Warfare, NWC 1032B, Newport, RI: US Naval War College, 2011.

26 Davis Lance E. and Engerman Stanley L., 2006, *Naval Blockades in Peace and War: An Economic History Since 1750*, Cambridge: Cambridge University Press, p. 453.

27 Barnett Roger W, Technology and Naval Blockade: Past Impact and Future Prospects, *Naval War College Review*, Vol. 58, No. 3 (Summer 2005), pp. 87-98.

IV

Mine Warfare

Mine warfare is the strategic, operational and tactical use of sea mines and the countermeasures to defeat them. The concept of a sea mine can be traced to "Greek Fire" used to defend Constantinople in the year 673. Naval mines were used in several conflicts during the nineteenth century, including the Crimean War, the American Civil War, the war between Russia and Turkey in 1877–78 and the war between China and France in 1884–85. Naval mines were used extensively during the Russo-Japanese War of 1904-1905, particularly during the blockade of Port Arthur by the Japanese. During the blockade, the Japanese were able to augment their ships by laying a field of electro-mechanical mines on the nights of April 12th and 13th which would eventually claim the life of Admiral Makarov, Commander of the Russian Pacific Squadron.[1] World War I witnessed the largest use of mines as the US and Great Britain deployed nearly 72,000 mines, called the North Sea Barrage. One of the earliest British naval losses in the First World War occurred when HMS Audacious, a King George V-class battleship, struck a naval mine in October 1914. Despite being one of the most modern ships in the Royal Navy, the vessel was no match for a relatively simple naval mine and sank after striking the mine, without ever being involved in operations against the enemy.[2] Korea, Vietnam, the Falklands Campaign, and the Gulf Wars among others, are conflicts in more recent times in which naval mines were used to alter the course of events.[3] In the ongoing war, Russia and Ukraine have accused each other of laying naval mines recently found in the Black Sea.

1 Russo-Japanese War, 11th edition, Encyclopaedia Britannica, Vol. 23, pp. 919-930.

2 Letts David, Naval Mines: Legal considerations in armed conflict, *International Review of the Red Cross*, Vol. 88(2), 2016, pp. 543–565.

3 Rios John J., Naval Mines in the 21STCentury: Can NATO Navies meet the Challenge? Masters' Thesis, Naval Postgraduate School, California, June 2005, p. 61.

Naval mines are unique weapons in terms of both their design and purpose. The naval mine is a relatively cheap, easy-to-employ, highly effective weapon that affords weaker navies the ability to oppose larger, more technologically advanced adversaries. Throughout naval war history, mine countermeasures attempted to keep pace with the development of new sea mines and the adaptation of counter-countermeasures on existing mines. There are more than a quarter-million sea mines of more than 300 types in the inventories of more than 50 navies worldwide, excluding the US.[4] Some 30 countries produce naval mines, and at least 20 countries export them to anyone with cash in hand.[5] This figure does not include underwater improvised explosive devices, which can be fashioned from fuel bladders, 50-gallon oil drums, and discarded refrigerators using commercially available or synthesized explosive material. Such weapons would have the inherent tactical and strategic advantages of naval mines. Mine hunting and clearance operations are dangerous and time-consuming, even after hostilities have ceased. Mines can directly attack the nation's waterborne trade.

Classification of Naval Mines

There have been numerous developments in naval mine technologies, both in terms of offensive and defensive capabilities. At the same time, old mines can be refitted with modern, highly sophisticated components, and any mine can be equipped with counter-countermeasure features—e.g., "ship counts"—to frustrate sweeping, hunting, and neutralization. They can be fabricated from fiberglass and plastic, making them extremely difficult to detect, identify, or counter once in the water. There are several different ways to classify mines, including how they are deployed, how they are situated in the water column, and how they are actuated. Naval mines can be broadly categorized into six different types:[6]

4 Reportedly, the US Navy has stockpiled fewer than 10,000 dedicated mines—including a "handful" of Mk-67 Submarine-Launched Mobile Mines (SLMMs) that can be deployed only on the remaining Improved *Los Angeles*-class (I688) attack submarine, and "Quick-strike" (QS) mine-conversion kits for general-purpose bombs. Brett Tingley, Navy Offers Gimps of its Submarine-Launched Capabilities in the Mediterranean, The War Zone, June 28, 2021.

5 US Navy, 21st Century US Navy Mine Warfare: Ensuring Global Access and Commerce, Programme Executive Office for Littoral and Mine Warfare, Expeditionary Warfare Directorate, June 2009, pp. 7-8.

6 International Law Applicable to Naval Mines, Chatham House, The Royal Institute of International Affairs, October 2014, p. 9.

- **Moored mines** are those tethered to the bottom of the sea bed by an anchor and hover beneath the surface of the sea. They usually detonate on contact with a vessel. Their design is such that they are typically limited to emplacement in waters shallower than 200 metres. Once their location is identified, they are relatively easy to sweep even with unsophisticated minesweepers, although such operations can be time-consuming.[7]

- **Drifting or floating mines** can be deployed in any depth of water. Once deployed, the mine-laying state typically has no control over them as they move with currents or prevailing weather conditions. Accordingly, they present the most risk of damaging unintended targets (including the ships of the mine-laying state).[8]

- **Bottom mines** are technologically advanced mines that rest on the sea bed and operate based on magnetic, electric, acoustic or pressure signatures of passing vessels. They are normally only effective in waters shallower than 200 metres. Such mines are designed to be armed or disarmed remotely and can be programmed to self-destruct. In contrast to drifting or floating mines, they are hard to sweep, dismantle and remove.

- **Remotely controlled mines** are technologically advanced mines that can be both deactivated and reactivated by coded acoustic signals. Technically, any of the mines described above could be made remote controlled but, in practice, the less sophisticated moored/floating mines rarely are.

---

7 There are three types of moored mines: close-tethered mines near the sea floor, in-volume mines, and near-surface mines. Moored mines require a large internal air space to allow the mine case to become buoyant, which limits the quantity of explosives that they can contain. As a result, the damage radius of a moored mine is generally less than that of a bottom mine. Some moored mines, however, are armed with torpedoes or rockets that greatly increase the reach of weapons against submerged and surface targets.

8 On April 14, 1987, during the Tanker War in the Arabian Gulf, the guided-missile frigate USS Samuel B. Roberts almost sank after striking an Iranian contact mine that was based on a 1908 Russian design. The mine blew a 15-foot hole in the hull, flooded the engine room, and knocked the two gas turbines from their mounts. The blast also broke the keel of the ship. Estimated to cost about $1,500, the mine caused some $96 million in damage to the warship. Repaired and returned to duty, the ship served until decommissioned in 2015. *How We Fight: Handbook for the Naval Warfighter*, Government Printing Office, October 15, 2015, p. 42.

- **Submarine-launched mobile mines** are mines that operate in much the same manner as bottom mines but are placed on the sea bed employing a torpedo launched from a submarine. They are designed to be laid in target areas that are difficult to reach including inner harbours, dockyards and up rivers.

- **Rising or rocket mines** are high-technology mines moored to the bottom of the sea bed. They may be employed to depths as great as 2,000 metres. They are usually designed for use against submarines and are programmed to release either a floating or fired payload, based on specific targeting criteria.

Drifting mines have accounted for much of the damage experienced by merchant vessels during the mining of the Suez Canal and the Red Sea (allegedly by Libya) in 1984 and during the Iran-Iraq Tanker Wars in the 1980s. Limpet mines can be attached by miners directly to the hull of an intended ship target, and they can be set to explode minutes or days or longer after being put in place. For example, in July 1985 two timed-delay limpet mines sank the Greenpeace Rainbow Warrior in the Auckland, New Zealand harbour.

Methods of Actuation

The most important classification standard for mines is the method of actuation. The three basic methods of actuation are contact, influence, and remote-actuated. Contact mines are normally moored or drifting and have either chemical horns or galvanic antennas that fire the mine when the horns or antenna come in contact with the hull of a ship. Contact mines are the oldest, simplest, and cheapest available to developing nations. Unlike contact mines, influence mines are actuated when the weapon detects a specific influence parameter by a passing vessel. These can be magnetic, acoustic, seismic, pressure, underwater electric potential, remote-controlled, or a combination of any of the above. Multi-influence sensors make it much more difficult for countermeasures to be effectively employed against these mines and can be further complicated by the addition of ship counters and delayed-arming features. Remote-actuated mines are like improvised explosive devices (IEDs) that may not be able to be countered with influence sweeps. The danger of remote-actuated mines lies in the fact that a third party could detonate the mines at will, particularly when

Mine Countermeasures (MCM)[9] forces are in the process of exploiting the mines.[10] Such Command-detonated mines are moored or bottom weapons that are fired on order by the miner when the target ship enters the minefield. Command-detonated minefields are generally limited to defensive operations in harbours or restricted waterways.[11]Clearing mines is a slow, extremely dangerous process.

International Law Applicable to Naval Mines and Interpretations

Naval mines have been deployed in almost every maritime conflict over the last hundred years or so. They form a key part of the naval weapons inventory of several states. The 1982 United Nations Convention on the Law of the Sea (UNCLOS) does not expressly refer to mine-laying or, for that matter, the right of states to undertake mine countermeasure (MCM) operations. However, UNCLOS is the most relevant treaty for determining the circumstances under which a state may lawfully lay mines in peacetime. The extensive and uncontrolled use of naval mines by both sides in the Russo-Japanese War of 1904–1905 inflicted great damage on innocent shipping during and long after that conflict and led to the 1907 Hague Convention VIII Relative to the Laying of Automatic Submarine Contact Mines.[12]

9 Naval mine countermeasures (MCM) programmes for countermine warfare employ a mix of undersea, surface, and airborne systems (including special warfare, marine mammal, and explosive ordnance disposal units). The resulting capabilities, together with support from other command, control, communications, computing, intelligence, surveillance, and reconnaissance (C4ISR) systems, are intended to provide the naval forces with minefield intelligence, surveillance, and reconnaissance (ISR) to facilitate minefield avoidance, minefield clearance, mine neutralization, and mine and obstacle removal and destruction. Their operational utility depends also on access to key environmental data, and modelling and simulation systems. *Naval Mine Warfare: Operational and Technical Challenges for Naval Forces*, 2001, National Research Council, Washington, DC: The National Academies Press, p. 217.

10 Rios John J., Naval Mines in the 21STCentury: Can NATO Navies meet the Challenge? Masters' Thesis, Naval Postgraduate School, California, June 2005, p. 61.

11 The Commander's Handbook on the Law of Naval Operation, The US Navy, Marine Corps, and Coast Guard, March 2022, Para 9.2.

12 Convention No. VIII, Relative to the Laying of Automatic Submarine Contact Mines, October 18, 1907.

The Hague Convention VIII

Article 1 of the Hague Convention VIII states that it is forbidden to lay unanchored automatic contact mines, except when they are so constructed as to become harmless one hour at most after the person who laid them ceases to control them. It also forbids laying of anchored automatic contact mines which do not become harmless as soon as they have broken loose from their moorings. In addition, torpedoes which do not become harmless when they have missed their mark, are not to be used.

Article 2 forbids Lying of automatic contact mines off the coast and ports of the enemy, with the sole object of intercepting commercial shipping. When anchored automatic contact mines are employed, every possible precaution must be taken for the security of peaceful shipping. The belligerents undertake to do their utmost to render these mines harmless within a limited time, and, should they cease to be under surveillance, to notify the danger zones as soon as military exigencies permit, by a notice addressed to ship owners, which must also be communicated to the Governments through the diplomatic channel.[13]

Article 4 of the Convention lays down responsibility for neutral powers. It states that neutral powers which lay automatic contact mines off their coasts must observe the same rules and take the same precautions as are imposed on belligerents. The neutral Power must inform ship owners, by a notice issued in advance, where automatic contact mines have been laid. This notice must be communicated at once to the Governments through the diplomatic channel. As regards the removal of mines, Article 5 states that at the close of the war, the Contracting Powers undertake to do their utmost to remove the mines which they have laid, each Power removing its mines. As regards anchored automatic contact mines laid by one of the belligerents off the coast of the other, their position must be notified to the other party by the Power which laid them, and each Power must proceed with the least possible delay to remove the mines in its waters.

San Remo Manual

The provisions of Hague VIII apply to automatic contact mines and do not apply strictly to other naval mines. However, the San Remo Manual provides that there are some basic principles which derive from Hague

13 Article 3, Convention No. VIII, Relative to the Laying of Automatic Submarine Contact Mines, October 18, 1907.

VIII and customary international law that relates to the law regarding naval mine warfare. These key principles are:

- Mines may only be used to achieve a legitimate military purpose;
- Belligerents must retain some control over mines they have deployed and/or can render a mine safe if such control is lost;
- Free-floating mines are forbidden unless they are directed against a military objective and they become harmless within an hour after control over the mine is lost;
- Notification of minefields must occur;
- The location of a minefield must be recorded so that the area can be cleared once hostilities have ceased; and
- Belligerents are not permitted to deploy mines in neutral waters or to use mines in a way that will have the practical effect of preventing passage between neutral waters and international waters.[14]

The US Navy Commander's Handbook

The US Navy Commander's Handbook states that armed mines may not be emplaced in international waters before the outbreak of armed conflict, except under the most demanding requirements of individual or collective self-defence. Should armed mines be emplaced in international waters under such circumstances, prior notification of their location must be provided. A nation emplacing armed mines in international waters during peacetime must maintain an on-scene presence in the area sufficient to ensure appropriate warning is provided to ships approaching the danger area. All armed mines must be expeditiously removed or rendered harmless when the imminent danger that prompted their emplacement has passed.[15]

The US Handbook states that during an armed conflict, naval mines may be lawfully employed by parties to an armed conflict subject to the following restrictions:

1. International notification of the location of emplaced mines must be made as soon as military exigencies permit.

14 Letts David, Beyond Hague VIII: Other Legal Limits on Naval Mine Warfare, *International Law Studies*, Vol. 90, 2014, pp. 446-474.

15 The Commander's Handbook on the Law of Naval Operation, The US Navy, Marine Corps, and Coast Guard, March 2022, Para 9.2.2.

2. Mines may not be emplaced by belligerents in neutral waters.
3. Anchored mines must become harmless as soon as they have broken their moorings.
4. Unanchored mines not otherwise affixed or embedded in the bottom (seabed) must become harmless within 1 hour after loss of control over them.
5. The location of minefields must be carefully recorded to ensure accurate notification and facilitate subsequent removal and/or deactivation.
6. Naval mines may be employed to channelize neutral shipping, but not in a manner to deny transit passage of international straits or archipelagic sea lanes passage of archipelagic waters by such shipping.
7. Naval mines may not be emplaced off the coasts and ports of the enemy with the sole objective of intercepting commercial shipping. They may otherwise be employed in the strategic blockade of enemy ports, coasts, and waterways.
8. It is prohibited to mine areas of indefinite extent in international waters. Reasonably limited barred areas may be established by naval mines provided neutral shipping retains an alternate route around or through such an area with reasonable assurance of safety.[16]

Legal Battles

The use of naval mines has been featured prominently in three key decisions of the International Court of Justice (ICJ): the *Corfu Channel case*, the *Nicaragua case*, and the *Oil Platforms* case.[17] The important principles which emerged from these cases affecting the use of naval mines are:

- A coastal State may deploy mines in its territorial waters in times of peace but in so doing it must not allow an unreported danger to

16 The Commander's Handbook on the Law of Naval Operation, The US Navy, Marine Corps, and Coast Guard, March 2022, Para 9.2.3.

17 These cases are: the Corfu Channel case, *UK v. Albania*, 1949, I.C.J., 4, April 9, 1949; Military and Paramilitary Activities in and against Nicaragua, *Nicaragua v. US*, 1986, I.C.J., 14, June 27, 1986; and Oil Platforms case (*Iran v. US*), 2003, I.C.J., 161, November 6, 2003.

shipping to exist.

- There is no unilateral right available to a state which would permit its military forces to enter another State's territorial sea and conduct mine-clearing operations in the absence of coastal State consent.[18]

- A positive obligation is placed upon a state to ensure that its waters are not used by other States (or organizations - including non-State actors) in a manner that would present a danger to vessels which are legitimately using those waters.

- Under customary international law, there is an obligation not to use force against another State, not to intervene in the internal affairs of another State, not to violate the sovereignty of another State and not to interrupt peaceful maritime commerce.[19]

- In peacetime, a state is prohibited from laying mines of any type in the territorial seas, internal waters or the archipelagic waters of another state. To do so would violate the territorial sovereignty of the latter and constitute the use of force14 unless the mine-laying is done with the consent of that state.

- The mining of a single military vessel might be sufficient to bring into play the 'inherent right of self-defence'.[20]

---

18 The mine-clearing operation in the Corfu Channel was undertaken by British forces was found to have violated Albanian sovereignty and was therefore a breach of international law. The rationale which underpins this principle can now be found in Article 2 of the 1982 UN Convention on the Law of the Sea, which stipulates that a coastal State's sovereignty extends to the territorial sea - hence any activity in the territorial sea by other States would have to be in conformity with the legal rights over that area of sea which the coastal State possesses.

19 The US provided support in a number of ways to one of the armed groups, engaged in non-international armed conflict with the Nicaragua government. One element of the support provided by the US was the provision of assistance by deploying naval mines in the internal waters and the territorial sea of Nicaragua. It was found by the ICJ that the US had breached its international legal obligations under customary international law by failing to disclose the existence and the location of the mines it had laid in the waters of Nicaragua.

20 However, in view of all the circumstances of the case, the ICJ was unable to conclude that the US was justified in using force in self-defence against the two Iranian oil platforms. In reaching this conclusion, the Court was unwilling to accept the contention put forward by the US that the mine which struck the USS Samuel B. Roberts had been laid by Iran.

Current Operational Scenario and Implications

It is clear that in an international armed conflict, the use of naval mines in a manner which offends the operative parts of Hague Convention VIII, as discussed above, is prohibited. However, in the present day "Gray-Zone" operation there is a possibility of laying of naval mines in violation of the Hague Convention VIII. The main characteristics of Gray-Zone operations include the uncertain legal status of the conflict itself, lack of certainty regarding the status of participants and their objectives, and the predominant use of unconventional means and methods of warfare.[21]

MCM operations in peacetime are governed exclusively by the legal regime applicable in peacetime; in times of armed conflict MCM operations by neutral states are necessarily tempered by the rights of the belligerents and the relevant rules of the law of armed conflict.

Summation

The use of naval mines can be both a means and method of naval warfare. They can be used for area denial, coastal and harbour defence, anti-surface and anti-submarine warfare, and blockade. When used exclusively for defensive purposes (e.g., moored mines used in area denial or harbour defence) laying of naval mines is considered a method of naval warfare and does not constitute an attack. When directed against a military objective (e.g., free-floating mines designed to hit a specific target) use of naval mines is a means of naval warfare that qualifies as an attack and is subject to the rules and principles of targeting law. The principle of distinction requires means and methods of warfare that constitute an attack only to be directed at military objectives. Unless they do something to lose their protected status, civilians and civilian objects may not be attacked. Drifting armed contact mines is indiscriminate. They are incapable of being directed specifically at a military objective and therefore forbidden by the law of naval warfare.[22]

Mines are the ultimate asymmetric warfare weapon in naval operations. Whether buried, tethered, concealed, drifting or even a dummy, they can deny access to a choke point, harbour, amphibious landing site, or even

21 A Gray Zone "win" is not a win in the classic warfare sense. Votel Joseph L., Charles T. Cleveland, Charles T. Connett and Will Irwin, Unconventional Warfare in the Gray Zone, *Joint Force Quarterly*, Vol. 80, No. 1, 2016, pp. 101-109.

22 Pedrozo Raul (Pete), Russia-Ukraine Conflict: The War at Sea, International Law Studies, Volume 100, 2023, pp. 1-62.

to deep water passages. They are very effective anti-access/area denial weapons.[23] The law relating to naval mines remains unsettled in respect of a few issues which need to be clarified. However, the legal norms associated with the use of naval mines in an armed conflict must not deviate from the four basic principles of the law of armed conflict: namely distinction,[24] proportionality, military necessity and humanity/unnecessary suffering.[25] It would be preferable to have a modern treaty governing the use of all types of naval mines for the sake of being able to refer to a clear legal regime that is relevant to the twenty-first century, the impact of customary international law and "other legal limits" on the use of naval mines in international armed conflict.[26]

The San Remo Manual of 1994 imposes certain restrictions on naval commanders which apply exclusively to international armed conflict. International law prohibits the belligerents to an international armed conflict (IAC) from laying mines in the territorial seas, internal waters, archipelagic waters and international straits overlapping the territorial seas of states not parties to the conflict. During peacetime, international law permits any state to remove mines laid on the high seas if they are a hazard to navigation. There is a positive duty on states that have laid mines on the high seas during an armed conflict to remove or render them harmless after the cessation of hostilities. If the mines cannot be removed or rendered harmless, then they may be marked temporarily by buoys until removal or neutralization is possible.

23 Developments in Sea Mine Technology and their Detection, Asia Pacific Defence Reporter, October 2019, pp. 56-58.

24 Naval mines are passive weapons that wait for an enemy to approach. Technological developments aside, the majority of naval mines are still incapable of distinguishing between legitimate targets and protected entities. In such circumstances, the provision of notice and warning can be seen as a fundamental requirement to ensure that the principle of distinction is observed. Stephens D.G. and Fitzatrick, Legal Aspects of the Contemporary Naval Mine Warfare, *Loyola of Los Angeles International and Comparative Law Review*, Vol. 21, No. 4, 1999, pp. 553-590.

25 Letts David, Naval Mines: Legal considerations in armed conflict, *International Review of the Red Cross*, Vol. 88(2), 2016, pp. 543–565.

26 Letts David, Beyond Hague VIII: Other Legal Limits on Naval Mine Warfare, *International Law Studies*, Vol. 90, 2014, pp. 446-474.

V

Maritime Interdiction

Interdiction Operations, in general, are operations to divert, disrupt, delay, or destroy an enemy's surface capabilities before they can be used effectively against friendly forces, or to otherwise achieve objectives. According to NATO's publication on Maritime Interdiction Operation (MIO), Allied Tactical Publication (ATP): "A maritime interdiction operation (MIO) encompasses seaborne enforcement measures to intercept the movement of certain types of designated items into or out of a nation or specific area."[1] Fink (2016) has defined MIO as Naval operations that include the boarding, search and seizure of goods and the detention of persons on a foreign-flagged merchant vessel, outside the territorial jurisdiction of a State.[2]

The purpose of interdiction operations is to prevent adversaries from employing weaponry and reinforcing units at a time and place of their choosing. Interdiction can divert enemy forces or assets from areas where there are critical operational requirements for them.[3] When the threat emanates from the sea, a nation, at peace or war, may conduct MIO of vessels at sea to protect their national security from that threat.[4] These operations can range from a bridge-to-bridge query of the master of the

1 NATO Allied Technical Publication 71, Allied Maritime Interdiction Operation, 2005, 1-1.

2 Fink Martin, 2018, *Maritime Interception and the Law of Naval Operations: A study of legal bases and legal regimes in maritime interception operations*, The Hague: Springer, pp. 317, at p. 13.

3 Joint Interdiction, Joint Publication 3-03, US Marine Corps, Department of the Navy, September 9, 2016, p. vii.

4 Maritime interception operations, as opposed to maritime interdiction operations, are a form or subset of interdiction used for sanction enforcement that are military or legal in nature, and serve both political and military purposes. Joint Interdiction, Joint

vessel through stopping, boarding, searching or seizing the cargo or vessel to an all-out blockade by a belligerent in war. It can be used to enforce sanctions or national policies imposed unilaterally, multi-nationally, or as directed by the United Nations or other intergovernmental organisations or regional authorities.[5]

Interdiction operations can be conducted by all components of the joint force, employing both lethal and nonlethal means. During interdiction operations, components may support or be supported by another component commander to achieve theatre/operational area-wide interdiction objectives, or they may conduct interdiction operations as part of their component mission. MIO may include the following: (i) Sending armed boarding parties to visit merchant ships bound to, through, or out of a defined regional area; (ii) Examining boarded ships' crewmembers' papers, documentation, and cargo; (iii) Searching for evidence of contraband, including weapon of mass destruction (WMD) or material required in the production of weapon of WMD; (iv) Diverting vessels failing to comply with the guidelines set forth by the sanctioning body or nation; (v) Seizing suspect vessels and their cargo that refuse to divert, and (vi) Destroying vessels and cargo, if necessary.

Maritime interdiction has been used by nations at war and during periods of tensions or hostilities not amounting to war to prevent enemies from moving forces or supplies or engaging in commerce to fund their military efforts. In December 2002, a multinational coalition of ships patrolling the coast of Pakistan for terrorists fleeing Afghanistan began tracking a merchant vessel *So San* registered in North Korea. The freighter was tracked for several days across the Indian Ocean and the Arabian Sea. As the freighter approached Yemen, Spanish and US forces intercepted and searched it on December 9, 2002. It was carrying a shipment of 15 Scud missiles and related cargo, buried beneath sacks of cement, which the Yemeni government had purchased from North Korea. The shipment was turned over to the US Navy. Yemen protested the ship's seizure and in a letter to the US stated that it had purchased the missiles for defensive

Publication 3-03, US Marine Corps, Department of the Navy, September 9, 2016, pp. I-8.

5 Smart Stephanie M., "Maritime Interdiction Operations," in Corn S. Geoffrey, Rachel E. VanLandingham and Shane R. Reeves, (ed), 2015, *US Military Operations: Law, Policy, and Practice*, Oxford: Oxford University Press, pp. 729-756.

purposes. The ship was ultimately allowed to proceed with missiles.[6] The reasons for its release were that import of the missiles did not violate any law, and the imported missile technology was so antiquated it presented only a very minimal threat to international security. In a statement by White House Spokesman, Ari Fleisher, the administration attributed the release of the shipment due to a failure of international law to prohibit Yemen from accepting delivery of the missile as neither Yemen nor North Korea was bound by the voluntary guidelines of the Missile Technology Control Regime.[7]

According to the Indian Navy, the MIO is undertaken to stop the movement of vessels that jeopardise India's maritime security interests, to prevent their reaching the intended destination. The conduct of MIO would be based on specific intelligence or security conditions and under applicable laws, to prevent or counter movement of maritime threats in the region. This may include operations in support of friendly nations on their request to the Government of India. These operations may be conducted independently, in joint action with the Indian Coast Guard and other armed forces, or coordination with maritime forces of friendly countries.[8]

Maritime Narcotic Interdiction

In February 2022 a joint team of the Indian Navy and the Narcotics Control Bureau (NCB) seized 529 kg of Hashish, 221 kg of Methamphetamine and 13 kg of Heroin in the high seas off the coast of Gujarat. The seizure was part of Operation *Samudragupt* targeting maritime trafficking of drugs originating from Afghanistan and Baluchistan. The drugs had their origin in Pakistan and were loaded onto the mother ship from the Makran coast. A total of approximately 3200 kg of Methamphetamine, 500 kg of Heroin and 529 kg of Hashish seized in the operation so far.[9]

---

6 Kerr Paul, US Stops Then Releases Shipment of N. Korean Missiles, Arms Control Association, available at: https://www.armscontrol.org/act/2003-01/news/us-stops-then-releases-shipment-n-korean-missiles.

7 David Sanger and Thom Shanker, Threats and Responses: War Materiel; Reluctant US Gives Assent for Missiles to Go to Yemen, *New York Times*, December 12, 2002.

8 Ensuring Secure Seas: Indian Maritime Security Strategy, Integrated Headquarters, Ministry of Defence (Navy), 2015, pp. 185, at p. 100.

9 Seizure of approximately 2500kg high purity Methamphetamine sourced from Death crescent valued around Rs. 15,000 Cr in the Indian waters. Press Information Bureau, Thiruvananthpuram, May 13, 2013. NCB, Indian Navy makes biggest ever drug haul, *The Hindu*, May 13, 2023.

A large number of MIO have been conducted in support of the United Nations resolutions in various parts of the globe. Today, MIO has been expanded to include interdiction of individuals, called Leadership Interception Operations (LIO), who are associated with al-Qaida, the Taliban, or other terrorist organisations.[10]

Legality for MIO

Belligerent Right to Conduct MIO

During an armed conflict, belligerents have a right under the law of armed conflict to undertake MIO.[11] According to Pyke (1915), "The right of visiting and searching merchant ships upon the high seas, whatever be the ships, whatever be the cargoes, whatever be the destinations, is an incontestable right of the lawfully commissioned cruisers of a belligerent nation ... the right is equally clear in practice, for practice is uniform and universal upon the subject.[12] MIO would aim to isolate an enemy from outside support, halt undesired maritime activity, provide security for other naval operations, and ensure the availability of the sea lines of communication for friendly operations such as the deployment of forces. The primary belligerent rights implicated by maritime interdiction are the right to visit and search and the right to the blockade. A belligerent right to visit and search allows a belligerent to stop all enemy or neutral vessels

10 Expanded maritime interception operations (EMIO) are authorized by the President and directed by the Secretary of Defence to deter, degrade, and/or disrupt or gather raw intelligence to potentially prevent attacks against the US and its allies. EMIO involves interception of vessels identified to be transporting targeted personnel or materiel that pose an imminent threat to the US and its allies. EMIO may be implemented without sanctions and may involve multinational forces or other USG departments and agencies. Joint Interdiction, Joint Publication 3-03, US Marine Corps, Department of the Navy, September 9, 2016, pp. II-4.

11 The law of naval warfare is a specialized subset of rules in the law of armed conflict that applies during international armed conflict at sea. They regulate naval warfare issues such as blockades, contraband, hospital ships and the protection of wounded and shipwrecked at sea. It also includes the law of maritime neutrality. The law of naval warfare also contains the belligerent right of visit and search. There is no modern treaty that explicitly codifies this right, although it is implied in some provisions of the law of naval warfare. The belligerent right of visit and search is however a longstanding and accepted right for States during international armed conflict. Fink Martin, 2018, *Maritime Interception and the Law of Naval Operations: A study of legal bases and legal regimes in maritime interception operations*, The Hague: Springer, pp. 317, at p. 166.

12 Pyke H.R., 1915, *The Law of Contraband of War*, Oxford: Clarendon Press, pp. 196-197.

from entering or exiting specific ports or coastal areas of an enemy nation, outside of neutral waters, to determine the true character of the vessels to interdict the flow of contraband goods. This right does not permit the search and visit of warships. The San Remo Manual in Rule 118 states that in order to exercise the right to visit during a conflict, reasonable grounds for suspicion must exist. The commentary to Rule 118 adds that 'The right of visit and search may not be exercised arbitrarily. An unrestricted practice of visit and search has never been considered to be in accordance with international law.'[13] The belligerent rights to MIO must be undertaken respecting principles of necessity, proportionality, and discrimination.

MIO under the UNCLOS

The UNCLOS guarantees freedom of navigation on the high seas, and protects the rights of transit passage and innocent passage for vessels in international straits and the territorial waters of other nations, respectively. These freedoms ensure a vessel's undisturbed movement through the seas, subject to only limited exceptions. Further, innocent passage through the territorial seas of other nations is inalienable so long as it is not prejudicial to the peace, good order or security of the coastal state.

UNCLOS provides a legal basis for conducting an MIO. Stateless vessels, or ships of uncertain nationality, may be subject to boarding and searching by all nations' navies or coast guards. Stateless vessels are vessels that are not legitimately registered in any one state. They are not entitled to fly the flag of any nation and are not entitled to the protection of any state's sovereignty. Therefore, if a suspect vessel is determined to be stateless on the high seas, a warship may visit and board the vessel without the consent of the master.[14] Naval forces or coast guard authorities may stop and search a flagged ship on the high seas when that ship is suspected of slave trading, piracy, illicit narcotics trafficking, and unauthorised broadcasting. These crimes are specifically enumerated in UNCLOS Article 110, and if there are reasonable grounds to believe that a ship is engaged in any of these crimes, personnel from a warship may board the suspect vessel on the high seas without the consent of the flag state or the master.

13 Rule No. 118 of San Remo Manual reads: In exercising their legal rights in an international armed conflict at sea, belligerent warships and military aircraft have a right to visit and search merchant vessels outside neutral waters where there are reasonable grounds for suspecting that they are subject to capture.

14 Article 110, UNCLOS.

MIO in Self-Defence

Article 51 of the UN Charter restates the inherent right of a state to defend itself from armed attack. The use of force in self-defence must meet the criteria of necessity and proportionality. Self-defence has been used by nations engaged in armed conflict as a legal basis to stop and search a foreign-flagged vessel suspected of carrying weapons to a party to the conflict. The US considers that it is still engaged in an armed conflict with the Taliban, al-Qaida, and affiliates, and thus continues to conduct MIOs in furtherance of this armed conflict.[15]

There are two sets of reasons that may render the use of force by maritime law enforcement agents permissible:

(a) Self-defence: The use of force that is reasonable and necessary in the circumstances of an attack or imminent attack upon law enforcement officials or others whom they have a right or obligation to protect from such harm, to stop or deter that attack or imminent attack. This is also referred to as individual self-defence and defence of others.

(b) Law enforcement purposes: Those purposes which are authorised by a relevant law or regulation of the authorising State of the maritime law enforcement agent and which permit the use of force in order to accomplish the specified law enforcement task or purpose.[16]

The use of deadly force in self-defence is only available in situations where the person has a reasonably objective belief that a threat poses an imminent danger of death or serious bodily harm to that person or others. However, when direct fire into a suspect vessel is used, it must be preceded by express warnings to that effect.

15 Smart Stephanie M., "Maritime Interdiction Operations," in Corn S. Geoffrey, Rachel E. VanLandingham and Shane R. Reeves, (ed), 2015, *US Military Operations: Law, Policy, and Practice*, Oxford: Oxford University Press, p. 729-756, at p. 742.

16 Examples of law enforcement purposes for which the use of force is authorized often include: (i) Stopping a suspect vessel; (ii) Boarding a suspect vessel; (iii) Searching a suspect vessel, its cargo and the people on board the vessel; (iv) Restraining or detaining people on board the vessel; (v) Seizing cargo or other items found on board the vessel; (vi) Cutting or destroying certain items found on board or deployed from the vessel (e.g. nets which cannot be recovered for some reason); (vii) Detaining the vessel; (viii) Controlling the vessel so as to steam or sail it to a port for further investigation.

MIO and Security Council Resolutions

Several MIO has been authorised under UN Security Council Resolutions (UNSCR) on the grounds of self-defence or collective self-defence. Chapter VII of the UN Charter allows the Security Council to determine the existence of any threat to the peace, breach of the peace, or act of aggression and to make recommendations or to resort to nonmilitary and military action to "maintain or restore international peace and security."[17] Article 41 of the Charter gives the Security Council the authority to use a variety of measures to enforce its decisions. The Security Council may decide what measures not involving the use of armed force are to be employed to give effect to its decisions, and it may call upon the Members of the United Nations to apply such measures; which do not involve the use of armed forces.

When the Security Council determines that Article 41 measures would be or have been inadequate; it may invoke Article 42 and take such action by air, sea, or land forces as may be necessary to maintain or restore international peace and security, including MIO. There have been Security Council Resolutions that have permitted the interdiction or embargo of goods. These include UNSCR 665 (1990), to authorise the maritime enforcement of economic sanctions against Iraq, to halt all inward and outward maritime shipping, and to inspect and verify their cargoes and destinations.[18] In Resolution 1973 (2011), the Security Council authorised MIO to enforce the arms embargo and support NATO operations in Libya by calling on member states to inspect their territory, including seaports and airports, and on the high seas, vessels and aircraft bound to or from Libya. With the increasing attempts to export oil by armed groups, the Security Council adopted Resolution 2146 (2014) to prevent the illicit export of crude oil from Libya. As Libya became the main transit country for migrant

17 Article 39, The United Nations Charter.

18 Resolution 665(1990) on the sanctions regime in relation to Iraq/Kuwait: Having decided in resolution 661 (1990) to impose economic sanctions under Chapter VII of the Charter of the United Nations, ... 1. [The Security Council] Calls upon those Member States cooperating with [Kuwait] which are deploying maritime forces to the area to use such measures commensurate to the specific circumstances as may be necessary under the authority of the Security Council to halt all inward and outward maritime shipping, in order to inspect and verify their cargoes and destinations and to ensure strict implementation of the provisions relating to such shipping laid down in resolution 661 (1990).

smuggling and human trafficking to Europe, the Security Council adopted Resolution 2240 (2015) which authorised UN Member States and regional organisations that are engaged in the fight against migrant smuggling and human trafficking to inspect on the high seas off the coast of Libya vessels suspected of being involved in migrant smuggling and human trafficking.[19] To enforce the arms embargo on Somalia, the Security Council has adopted Resolution 2662(2022) to reauthorise maritime interdiction of illicit weapons imports, charcoal exports, and improvised explosive device components.[20]

The modern laws of armed conflict at sea first require neutral merchant ships to submit to the belligerent right to visit and search during armed conflict outside neutral waters. Visit, search and seizure are rights exercisable only by belligerent war vessels (or helicopters). The belligerent must have reasonable grounds for suspecting that the neutral ship is subject to capture for the carriage of contraband, breach of blockade or other un-neutral service. The 'reasonable grounds' requirement is founded

19 Para 7 and 8 of the Resolution are as follows: 7. [The Security Council] Decides, with a view to saving the threatened lives of migrants or of victims of human trafficking on board such vessels as mentioned above, to authorize, in these exceptional and specific circumstances, for a period of one year from the date of the adoption of this resolution, Member States, acting nationally or through regional organizations that are engaged in the fight against migrant smuggling and human trafficking, to inspect on the high seas off the coast of Libya vessels that they have reasonable grounds to suspect are being used for migrant smuggling or human trafficking from Libya, provided that such Member States and regional organizations make good faith efforts to obtain the consent of the vessel's flag State prior to using the authority outlined in this paragraph; 8. Decides to authorize for a period of one year from the date of the adoption of this resolution, Member States acting nationally or through regional organizations to seize vessels inspected under the authority of paragraph 7 that are confirmed as being used for migrant smuggling or human trafficking from Libya, and underscores that further action with regard to such vessels inspected under the authority of paragraph 7, including disposal, will be taken in accordance with applicable international law with due consideration of the interests of any third parties who have acted in good faith. Seyrafi Sassan, Enforcing UN Sanctions by Maritime Interdiction: Historical Overview and Legal Basis, *The Iranian Review for UN Studies (IRUNS)*, Vol.2, Issue 1, Winter & Spring 2019, pp. 153-203.

20 The Security Council has decided that all States will take the necessary measures to prevent all deliveries of weapons and military equipment to Somalia, including prohibiting the financing of all acquisitions and deliveries of weapons and military equipment and the direct or indirect supply of technical advice, financial and other assistance, and training related to military activities, except where the beneficiary is Somalia's security and police institutions at the national and local level, who are exempt.

on the fact that if there are no such grounds for suspicion, the exercise of these rights would not be necessary and proportionate for the belligerent's self-defence.[21]

MIO and Technology

The US Navy conducts thousands of MIOs every year to enforce embargoes, intercept contrabands, prevent drug and human smuggling, and fight piracy. These operations are usually conducted by eight-man Visit, Board, Search, and Seizure (VBSS) teams using rigid-hull inflatable boats (RHIBs) or helicopters, often operating miles from the base ship. Most boarding operations are "compliant" (the target ship complies with the Navy's order to stop, and lower a ladder for the boarding team), but a fair number are non-compliant, where orders are ignored. In this case, the VBSS RHIB has to match the speed of the suspect ship, and team members must board using rope ladders with grappling hooks. Once aboard, the VBSS team quickly secures the deck and the pilot house and then begins a sweep of the rest of the ship. One of the most dangerous operations during this phase is the descent into the hull of the ship. There is usually a ladder leading down into the bowels of the ship that is referred to as the "ladder of death." The US Navy is planning to acquire a small tactical robot that can be deployed ahead of the team to provide enhanced situational awareness in these boarding, breaching, and clearing operations.[22]

Summation

Maritime interdiction operations are well-founded in history and law as a means to counter threats from the sea. During the last few decades, MIO has become a well-established operational activity for navies all around the world. MIO has firmly established itself as one of the roles of navies and found its way also to the maritime doctrines of States and international organisations.[23] As a general rule of law and practice, maritime interdiction

21 Humphrey, D. R., Belligerent Interdiction of Neutral Shipping in International Armed Conflict, *Journal of Conflict and Security Law*, Vol. 2, No. 1, 1997, pp. 23-44.

22 Nguyen Hoa G. and Mendel Baker, Characteristics of a maritime interdiction operations unmanned ground vehicle, Report, Space and Naval Warfare Systems Centre Pacific, San Diego, April 2012, p. 8.

23 Fink Martin, 2018, *Maritime Interception and the Law of Naval Operations: A study of legal bases and legal regimes in maritime interception operations*, The Hague: Springer, p. 317.

operations can only be carried out by warships, other duly authorised government ships or military aircraft. Bilateral or regional ship boarding agreements have also been used to conduct maritime interdiction operations.

VI

Submarine Warfare

Submarine, in its earliest form when it was to be directed solely against warships, was considered a controversial weapon. From the very beginning of the idea of a vessel that would travel under the water instead of on the water, it was accepted that if it could be successfully developed it would be an asset to small nations, which could not afford large standing navies. It was assumed that, because of its anticipated short range, it would be used primarily for coastal defence. Modern nuclear-powered submarines are quite different from those used during the Second World War. Submarines could be used for three different purposes in modern warfare: reconnaissance, anti-ship operations and land attacks. In a territorial sea, a submarine has the right of innocent passage, provided it navigates on the surface and shows its true flag. The right of innocent passage also exists in archipelagic waters and adjacent territorial seas, and the submarine must navigate on the surface and fly its flag. If straits used for international navigation are overlapped by territorial seas, submarines may pass through the straits exercising the right of transit passage. In exclusive economic zones and the high seas, the submarine may operate submerged.

Submarines can either be diesel-electric or nuclear-powered. Either type can hold nuclear warheads. The nuclear-powered submarines have increased speed (allowing submerged submarines to keep up with fast surface ships) and operational radius (a nuclear submarine can patrol while submerged for weeks rather than hours).[1] Since the end of the Second

1 India's historic first nuclear-powered submarine, the indigenously developed INS Arihant, was commissioned in August 2016 at the Indian Navy's dockyard in Visakhapatnam, home to India's Eastern Naval Command.

World War, submarines have sunk only three warships: a frigate, a cruiser, and a corvette; and no merchant vessels.[2]

Legal Framework

Submarines are stealthy platforms which use torpedoes, missiles, and mines to attack enemy armed forces during armed conflict, targeting enemy submarines, surface ships, and naval auxiliaries. The main advantage of a submarine over a surface warship is its underwater capability. Militarily, this translates into the ability to hide from the enemy and the ability to approach a target from its hidden position to carry out surprise attacks. [3] The international rules governing the conduct of submarine warfare accommodated three branches of international law: the law of the sea, the law of neutrality, and the law regulating the conduct of military operations.[4] The fundamental principles of IHL that remain applicable in submarine warfare are (i) the right of the belligerent to adopt means of injuring the enemy is not unlimited; (ii) it is prohibited to launch an attack against the civilian population and civilian objects as such; and (iii) a distinction must be made between combatants and non-combatants, and non-combatants must be spared as much as possible. These principles govern the targeting in submarine warfare.

Submarine Targeting

Attack at Sea

IHL imposes essentially the same rules on submarines as those applying to surface warships. Submarines may employ their conventional weapons systems to attack enemy surface, subsurface or airborne targets wherever located beyond neutral territory. Enemy warships and military aircraft,

2 On March 26, 2010, a North Korean submarine torpedoed 1,200-tonne ROKN *Cheonan* (PCC- 772) a South Korean Navy corvette in the Yellow Sea. The ship broke into two from an explosion. The sinking took place only two km off Baengnyeong Island, South Korea's northwesternmost territory, and near the coastline of North Korea. Salvage operations confirmed that a North Korean heavy torpedo armed with a 200- kilogram warhead had struck the South Korean warship, killing 46 Navy sailors of the Republic of Korea (ROK). North Korean torpedo sank Cheonan, South Korea military source claims, *The Guardian*, April 10, 2010.

3 Jacobson Jon L., The Law of Submarine Warfare Today, *International Law Review*, Vol. 64, 1991, pp. 205-240.

4 Roach J. Ashley, Legal Aspects of Modern Submarine Warfare, *Max Planck Yearbook of United Nations Law*, Vol. 6, 2002, pp. 367-385.

including naval and military auxiliaries, may be attacked and destroyed without warning. The rules applicable to surface warships regarding enemy ships that have surrendered in good faith, or that have indicated their intention to do so, apply to submarines as well. In 1982, the Argentine cruiser *General Belgrano* was sunk by the British Churchill-class submarine *HMS Conqueror*, as it was a legitimate military objective. Commanders must take all reasonable precautions to keep civilian casualties and damage to civilian property to a minimum. The submarine commander must also consider the likely environmental damage which will result from an attack on a legitimate military objective.

Submarine Weaponry

The law of armed conflict or IHL prohibits the employment of weapons in such a manner as to cause excessive suffering or disproportionate risk of harm to noncombatants. Therefore, self-propelled torpedoes, the principal weapons of submarines, must disarm if they miss their targets. The US Commander's Handbook on Naval Operations states, "Missiles and projectiles dependent upon over-the-horizon or beyond-visual-range guidance systems are lawful, provided they are equipped with sensors or are employed in conjunction with external sources of targeting data, that is sufficient to ensure effective target discrimination."[5] In addition, the rules concerning the laying of stationary mines forbid their use in areas or manners that unduly endanger commercial shipping. Like other platforms that use these weapons, submarines must comply with the laws of war that govern them.

In the past decade, the perceived underwater warfare threat has grown. The desire to move away from older conventional diesel-powered submarines to much quieter, more powerful nuclear submarines has pushed maritime nations to continually invest in developing future Anti-Submarine Warfare (ASW) technologies. A new era is quickly emerging as the future of ASW: Autonomous Underwater Vehicles (AUV).

Enemy Merchant Shipping

The rules of naval warfare about submarine operations against enemy merchant shipping are one of the least developed areas of the IHL. Although the submarine's effectiveness as a weapons system is dependent upon its capability to remain submerged (and thereby undetected) and despite its vulnerability when surfaced, the London Protocol of 1936 makes

5 Ibid, Para 9.4.

no distinction between submarines and surface warships concerning attacks upon enemy merchant shipping. The London Protocol specifies that except in case of persistent refusal to stop when ordered to do so, or in the event of active resistance to capture, a warship "whether surface vessel or submarine" may not destroy an enemy merchant vessel "without having first placed passengers, crew and ship's papers in a place of safety". The London Protocol of 1936, coupled with the customary practice of belligerents during and following World War II, imposes upon submarines the responsibility to provide for the safety of passengers and crew, and the ship's papers before the destruction of an enemy merchant vessel unless:

- The enemy merchant vessel persistently refuses to stop when duly summoned to do so.
- It actively resists visit and search or capture.
- It is sailing under a convoy of enemy warships or enemy military aircraft.
- It is armed.
- It is incorporated into or is assisting in any way the enemy's military intelligence system.
- It is acting in any capacity as a naval or military auxiliary to an enemy's armed forces.

All ships, including submarines, must "take all possible measures" to search for and collect survivors after each engagement. If such humanitarian efforts would subject the submarine to undue additional hazard or prevent it from accomplishing its military mission, the location of possible survivors should be passed at the first opportunity to a surface ship, aircraft, or shore facility capable of rendering assistance. Firing upon shipwrecked survivors in the water is a war crime. In the *Lhdovery Castle Case* (1921), a German tribunal tried and convicted the officers of a U-boat for, "contrary to international law", firing upon and killing survivors of an unlawfully torpedoed hospital ship during World War I. In the *Peleus Case* (1946), a British tribunal tried and convicted the commanding officer of a German submarine that during World War II had systematically fired upon the survivors of a torpedoed merchant vessel as they clung to wreckage and rafts.

Neutral Merchant Ships

Flying a neutral flag does not establish the neutral character of a merchant ship. Neutral merchant vessels are subject to visit and search, but may not be captured or destroyed by submarines. Any merchant ship owned or controlled by a belligerent possesses enemy character, regardless of whether it is operating under a neutral flag or bears neutral marking. Vessels acquiring enemy character may be treated by an opposing belligerent as if they are, in fact, enemy vessels, and may be attacked. Neutral vessels may acquire enemy character when engaging in either of the following acts: (i) taking a direct part in the hostilities on the side of the enemy, (ii) acting in any capacity as a naval or auxiliary to the enemy's armed forces, (iii) operating directly under enemy control or directions, and (iv) resisting an attempt to establish identity, including visit and search. The San Remo Manual states that merchant vessels flying the flag of a neutral State may not be attacked unless they:

- Are believed to be carrying contraband or breaching a blockade, and after warning intentionally refusing to stop, or intentionally resisting visit and search.
- Engage in belligerent acts on behalf of the enemy.
- Act as auxiliaries to the enemy's armed forces.
- Sail under convoy of enemy warships or military aircraft.
- Make an effective contribution to the enemy's military action.

The US Commander's Handbook on the Law of Naval Operations (NWP 1-14M) includes references to the laws of naval warfare that specifically address the submarine weapons system and also rules that apply or can apply, to submarines and their roles in wartime. The Handbook states that submarines may employ their weapons systems to attack enemy surface, subsurface, or airborne targets wherever located beyond neutral territory. Enemy warships and military aircraft, including naval and military auxiliaries, may be attacked and destroyed without warning. Rules applicable to surface warships regarding enemy ships that have surrendered in good faith, or have indicated their intention to do so, apply to submarines. To the extent that military exigencies permit, submarines are required to search for and collect the shipwrecked, wounded, and sick following an engagement. If such humanitarian efforts would subject the submarine to undue additional hazard, or prevent it from accomplishing its military mission, the location of possible survivors should be passed at the first opportunity to a surface ship, aircraft, or shore facility capable of rendering assistance.[6]

Exemptions from Submarine Interdiction

The specifically exempt vehicles include:

- Cartel vessels, i.e., those designated for and engaged in the exchange of POW.
- Properly designated and marked hospital ships, medical transports and medical aircraft.
- Vessels charged with religious, non-military scientific or philanthropic missions.
- Vessels guaranteed safe conduct by prior agreement between belligerents.
- Small coastal fishing vessels and small boats engaged in local coastal trade.
- Civilian passenger vessels are exempt from destruction but are subject to capture.

6 The Commander's Handbook on the Law of Naval Operations, Office of the Chief of Naval Operations, United States, March 2022, Para 8.7.

Section 3

Contemporary Complexities

VII

Maritime Autonomous Systems

The use of Unmanned Vehicles (UVs) to support naval operations is not a new phenomenon. During World War II unmanned marine vehicle (UMV)[1] technology appeared for the first time in smoke screen operations to clear mines.[2] Unmanned surface vessels (USV) were used in 1946 during Operation Crossroads by the US to investigate the effect of nuclear weapons on warships. The USVs were deployed to collect radioactive water samples after the two nuclear detonations at Bikini Atoll. During the Vietnam War, remotely controlled unmanned boats were used by the US Mine Division to conduct "chain drag" minesweeping operations. Similarly, in the 1990s, USS Cushing (DD-985) conducted remote mine-hunting operations in the Persian Gulf. Unmanned undersea/marine vehicles (UUVs or UMVs) were also used in 2003 to clear mines and conduct ISR missions in the

1 There are numerous types, technologies, and functions of unmanned underwater/maritime vehicles. Generally, UMVs are water-borne systems that are capable of operating without onboard personnel. UMVs are also commonly referred to as unmanned maritime systems (UMSs). As a result of most UMVs having some level of autonomy in order to operate without onboard personnel, some scholars use the term autonomous maritime vehicles (AMVs). Two subcategories of UMVs include unmanned undersea vehicles (UUVs) and unmanned surface vehicles (USVs). As the name indicates, UUVs operate primarily submerged and are far stealthier compared to USVs, though they typically need to surface for communications purposes. USVs are typically larger compared to UUVs and operate solely on water surfaces, resulting in more reliable and effective communications. USVs also have more payload capacity and endurance as compared to UUVs. Smaller UMVs include "floaters" and "gliders" that often conduct maritime scientific research, and UUVs are currently used for countermine operations and antisubmarine warfare. McCarl Lindsay I., Untethering UMVs from Vessels: Why the United States Should Construct a New Environmental Legal Scheme for Unmanned Maritime Vehicles, *Dickinson Law Review*, Vol. 127, Issue 2, 2022, pp. 469-524.

2 Bertram, V. *Unmanned Surface Vehicles—A Survey*; Copenhagen, Denmark, 2008; Volume 1, pp. 1–14.

Persian Gulf during Operation Iraqi Freedom.[3] In addition, Maritime Autonomous Vehicles (MAVs) have been increasingly used in oil spill removals, tested for cargo shipment, and in anti-terrorist operations. Saudi Arabia has intercepted remote-controlled boats carrying explosives and targeting an oil depot in Yemen for drug smuggling.

The use of maritime and aerial autonomous systems to support military operations has grown rapidly in the twenty-first century. They have attained prominence in terms of both the number of systems employed and the complexity and lethality of the missions they are assigned.[4] In the Syrian civil war, Russia has tested an Unmanned Underwater Vehicle. In the ongoing Russian-Ukraine armed conflict, the Russian military is testing new autonomous systems and technologies in almost every domain, including the sea.[5] The US Congress had recently approved two Large Unmanned Surface Vehicles (LUSVs), which could autonomously find their way to the fleet, expends missiles and work their way back to reload.[6]

---

3 US Department of the Navy, The Navy Unmanned Surface Vehicles (USV) Master Plan 1-3 (2007).

4 At present, more than 90 countries and non-state actors, including the Islamic State of Iraq and Syria (ISIS), operate surveillance or weaponized unmanned aerial systems in support of combat operations. Given that unmanned aerial systems have proven their ability in combat to enhance situational awareness, reduce human workload and improve mission performance, at reduced risk to both civilian and military personnel and reduced cost, we can expect the unmanned underwater vehicles would soon augment and support the manned fleet in select countries. Pedrozo Raul (Pete), "Unmanned and Autonomous Warships and Military Aircraft," in Kraska James and Park Young Kil, 2022, *Emerging technology and Law of the Sea*, UK: Cambridge University Press, pp. 347, at p. 273.

5 In February 2018, the Russian Military-Industrial Commission announced that the "Galtel" underwater "robotic complex" was engaged in the search for undersea unexploded ordnance; it also conducted sea-floor mapping and protection of the Tartus port area, where Russia has a naval base. Edmond Jeffrey and Samuel Bendett, Russian Military Autonomy in a Ukraine Conflict, CNA's Occasional Paper, February 2022, p. 12.

6 The US Navy has been developing and experimenting with various types of UUVs for many years. The US Navy wants to develop and acquire large, medium and extra-large Under Sea Vehicles as part of an effort to shift the Navy to a more distributed fleet architecture, meaning a mix of ships that spreads the Navy's capabilities over an increased number of platforms and avoids concentrating a large portion of the fleet's overall capability into a relatively small number of high-value ships. Ronald O'Rourke, Navy Large Unmanned Surface and Undersea Vehicles: Background and Issues for Congress, Congressional Research Service, April 17, 2023, p. 38.

System Configurations

Unmanned underwater vehicles (UUVs) can be equipped with sensors, weapons, or other payloads, and can be operated remotely, semi-autonomously, or autonomously. They can be individually less expensive to procure than manned ships and aircraft because their designs do not need to incorporate spaces and support equipment for onboard human operators. UUVs can be particularly suitable for long-duration missions that might tax the physical endurance of onboard human operators, or missions that pose a high risk of injury, death, or capture of onboard human operators[7], i.e., the five Ds - Detect, Designate, Dirty, Destructive and Dangerous.[8] In mid-October 2020, the US Navy conducted a successful test using a small quadcopter-type UAV to deliver supplies to an Ohio-class ballistic missile submarine, while deployed near the Hawaiian Islands. The test was conducted to explore new ways to resupply submarines at sea while they are on nuclear deterrent patrols to enhance their overall readiness.[9]

UUVs are force multipliers and risk-reduction systems that can assist naval forces in maintaining maritime superiority and control of the maritime battlespace. UUVs are employed in situations where they can increase performance at a lower cost to enable missions that cannot be performed by manned systems or reduce the risk to manned systems. They would provide an ideal platform to conduct dull missions that involve long-duration undertakings with mundane tasks that are ill-suited for manned systems, such as intelligence, surveillance and reconnaissance (ISR) missions. They can also better perform dirty missions, such as operations to detect chemical, biological and nuclear material, by significantly reducing the risk of exposure of personnel to hazardous conditions; and can be used

7 Ronald O'Rourke, Navy Large Unmanned Surface and Undersea Vehicles: Background and Issues for Congress, Congressional Research Service, April 17, 2023, p. 38.

8 Kishore Kumar Khera, Has the Time Come to Replace Manned Combat Aircraft with Armed Unmanned Aerial Vehicles? Available at https://idsa.in/idsacomments/replace-manned-combat-aircraft-with-armed-unmanned-aerial-vehicles_kkkhera_160817.

9 On October 19, 2020, a quad-copter-type drone delivered a small payload to the US Navy's Ohio Class ballistic missile submarine USS *Henry M. Jackson* as it sailed on the surface of the Pacific Ocean near Hawaii. The service said that this was a test to explore novel concepts for resupplying *Ohio* class submarines while they›re out on their nuclear deterrent patrols, but also brings up thoughts about how some aspects of at-sea replenishment, in general, may look in the future. Trevithick Joseph, The Navy Just Sent a Drone to Deliver Cargo to One of Its Ballistic Missile Submarines, TheDrive, October 21, 2020.

to conduct inherently dangerous missions, thereby reducing the risk of exposure to personnel.

Degree of Autonomy

According to the International Maritime Organization, Maritime Autonomous Surface Ships (MASS) refers to a ship which, to a varying degree, can operate independently of human interaction. The degree of autonomy has been distinguished as follows:

> **Degree 1: Ship with automated processes and decision support**: Seafarers are on board to operate and control shipboard systems and functions. Some operations may be automated and at times be unsupervised but with seafarers on board ready to take control.
>
> **Degree 2: Remotely controlled ship with seafarers on board:** The ship is controlled and operated from another location. Seafarers are available on board to take control and operate the shipboard systems and functions.
>
> **Degree 3: Remotely controlled ship without seafarers on board:** The ship is controlled and operated from another location. There are no seafarers on board.
>
> **Degree 4: Fully autonomous ship:** The operating system of the ship can make decisions and determine actions by itself. [10]

Legal Status of Unmanned Maritime Systems

The main issue relating to unmanned maritime systems (UMS) is whether they could be considered "ships" or "vessels" under international law. Further, those UMSs that can be considered "vessels" or "ships," can be considered "warships?" The definitions provided for ships and vessels do not address any issue as to whether there is a crew on board the ship or not.[11] While international law does not explicitly prohibit treating a

10 Maritime Autonomous Surface Ships: A critical 'MASS' for legislative review, UNCTAD, December 13, 2022, available at: https://unctad.org/news/transport-newsletter-article-no-97-fourth-quarter-2022.

11 The distinction has been relevant in the context of floats and gliders, which are autonomous vehicles or devices used for data collection. Some commentators have taken the view that small objects that float with currents with the sole purpose of collecting data and that are not subject to any navigation regime should be considered "equipment" under the regime for marine scientific research rather than as ships. Katharina Bork, et.al., The Legal Regulation of Floats and Gliders – In Quest of a New

UMS as a "vessel" or "ship," the law is designed with manned systems in mind. For example, UNCLOS Article 94, provides that "every State shall effectively exercise its jurisdiction and control in administrative, technical and social matters over ships flying its flag." This includes taking "measures for ships flying its flag" relating to vessel construction, equipment, seaworthiness, manning, crew training, effective communications, and the like "as are necessary to ensure safety at sea." These measures "shall include those necessary to ensure (i) that each ship is in the charge of a master and officers who possess appropriate qualifications, in particular in seamanship, navigation, communications and marine engineering, and that the crew is appropriate in qualification and numbers for the type, size, machinery and equipment of the ship; and (ii) that the master, officers and, to the extent appropriate, the crew are fully conversant with and required to observe the applicable international regulations concerning the safety of life at sea, the prevention of collisions, the prevention, reduction and control of marine pollution, and the maintenance of communications by radio."

Article 29 of UNCLOS defines a "warship" as: "a ship belonging to the armed forces of a State bearing the external marks distinguishing such ships of its nationality, under the command of an officer duly commissioned by the government of the State and whose name appears in the appropriate service list or its equivalent, and manned by a crew which is under regular armed forces discipline." The physical presence of a commander is not necessary to the legal conception of either command at sea, or of military command. The Australian Defence Force's definition of command is as follows: "The authority that a commander in the military service lawfully exercises over subordinates under rank or assignment. The command includes the authority and responsibility for effectively using available resources and for planning the employment of organizing, directing, coordinating and controlling military forces for the accomplishment of assigned missions."[12] The responsibility, coordination and direction of efforts as well as other related functions could be exercised remotely.[13]

Regime? *Ocean Development and International Law*, Vol. 39, Issue 3, 2008, pp. 298-328.

12 Australian Defence Doctrine Publication 00.1: Command and Control (2009) para 1.4.

13 Klein Natalie Klein, Guilfoyle D., Karim Md S. and McLaughlin Rob, Maritime Autonomous Vehicles: new frontiers in the law of the sea, *International Comparative Law Quarterly*, Vol. 69, issue 3, July 2020, pp. 719-734.

Unmanned aerial vehicles (UAVs) of the armed forces are considered military aircraft. Under customary international law, a "military aircraft" means any aircraft, which is (i) operated by the armed forces of a State; (ii) bearing the military markings of that State; (iii) commanded by a member of the armed forces, and (iv) controlled, manned, or preprogrammed by a crew subject to regular armed forces discipline. This definition was examined by a group of experts to provide commentary on the HPCR Manual on International Law Applicable to Air and Missile Warfare. Their analysis of the components of the definition of "military aircraft" is useful as it provided a contemporary example of how to interpret the term "vessel".[14]

If one were to apply the above interpretations of the law applicable to military aircraft to their maritime warships, a breakdown of the components found in Article 29's definition of "warship" yields the following conclusions: A warship must be a ship; (ii) The ship must belong to the armed forces of a State; and (iii) A warship is required to bear external marks indicating its Nationality; as long as the external marking denotes the ship's nationality and military purpose, the level of its discernibility should not matter; (iv) A warship has to be under the command of an officer duly commissioned by the government of the State and whose name appears on the appropriate service list. As long as a duly commissioned and listed officer exercises control over the vessel, his physical presence aboard the ship to exercise the necessary degree of control does not matter; and (v) A warship must be manned by a crew which is under regular armed forces discipline.[15] The "crew" does not have to be physical aboard a warship; the "manning" requirement is met concerning unmanned ships if the remote controllers

14 With regard to the stipulation that a military aircraft must be operated by the armed forces of a State, the aircraft need not 'belong" to the armed forces; an aircraft leased and operated by the armed forces, though still owned by the lessor, would qualify as a military aircraft. A military aircraft is required to bear the external markings of its State. These markings serve to both (1) clearly indicate the employment of the aircraft for military purposes, and thus distinguish it from other State aircraft, especially from police or customs aircraft, that are not used for military purposes; and (2) denote the nationality of the aircraft. A single mark may suffice to accomplish both purposes. The crux of the requirement is that there must be a marking. However, there is not a minimum threshold of discernibility; low visibility markings common with military aircraft today are satisfactory. As for the obligation that a military aircraft must be commanded by a member of the armed forces, the experts opined that that "commander" could either be on the craft itself or controlling it remotely. In other words, as long as a member of the armed forces exercised control over the aircraft, it was immaterial whether s/he was actually aboard the aircraft.

15 Article 29 of UNCLOS is replicated from1907 Hague Convention VII relating to the Conversion of Merchant Ships into War-Ships, October 18, 1907, Articles 2–6.

are individuals subject to regular armed forces control. Assuming the conclusions reached concerning military aircraft apply equally in the maritime realm, there is no absolute bar to a UMS meeting the "warship" requirements as set out in Article 29 of the UNCLOS.[16] UMS could be duly authorized by a government to exercise each of the peacetime rights enjoyed by warships, so long as it is marked accordingly and, crucially, qualifies as a ship.[17]

Legal Operational Limitations and Interpretation

Both the terms "passage" and "innocent" are defined in UNCLOS. "Passage" is defined as continuous and expeditious navigation through the territorial sea for either passing through without entering internal waters or heading to or from the internal waters of the coastal state.[18] The principal significance of "passage" is that ships are not allowed to linger in a coastal state's territorial sea. They are required to move continuously and expeditiously through the area. Passage is "innocent" so long as it is not prejudicial to the peace, good order or security of the coastal State.[19]

16 Norris Andrew, Legal Issues Relating to Unmanned Maritime Systems Monograph, The US Naval War College, 2013, p. 87.

17 Under UNCLOS, warship status affords certain rights. For instance, warships may seize a pirate ship (Article 107); visit a ship on the high seas suspected of engaging in piracy, the slave trade, unauthorized broadcasting, being without nationality, or flying a foreign flag (or showing no flag) when it is actually of the nationality of the ship conducting the visit (Article 110); conduct hot pursuit (Article 111(5)); and engage in enforcement measures designed to safeguard the marine environment Article 2240. Schmitt Michael N. and David S. Goddard, International law and the military use of unmanned maritime systems, *International Review of the Red Cross*, Vol. 98(2), 2016, pp. 567–592.

18 Articles 17 and 18, UNCLOS.

19 Article 19 of the UNCLOS, provides meaning of innocent passage: The activities which would be considered to be prejudicial to the peace, good order or security of the coastal State if engaged in in the territorial sea, are as follows: (a) any threat or use of force against the sovereignty, territorial integrity or political independence of the coastal State, or in any other manner in violation of the principles of international law embodied in the Charter of the United Nations; (b) any exercise or practice with weapons of any kind; (c) any act aimed at collecting information to the prejudice of the defence or security of the coastal State; (d) any act of propaganda aimed at affecting the defence or security of the coastal State; (e) the launching, landing or taking on board of any aircraft; (f) the launching, landing or taking on board of any military device; (g) the loading or unloading of any commodity, currency or person contrary to the customs, fiscal, immigration or sanitary laws and regulations of the coastal State; (h) any act of wilful and serious pollution contrary to UNCLOS; (i) any fishing activities; (j) the carrying out of research or survey activities; (k) any act aimed at interfering

On December 15, 2016, Chinese forces seized an unmanned underwater vehicle (UUV) being operated by a US government vessel, USNS Bowditch (an unarmed naval oceanographic vessel), nautical miles from the Philippine coast in the South China Sea. China did clarify the legality of its actions. The US government demanded the return of the UUV, which it said had been conducting routine operations following international law. The US claimed that it was a sovereign immune vessel of the US government. The Bowditch incident was finally resolved peacefully, with the return of the device some five days later. However, it raised legal issues such as the navigational rights and obligations of unmanned systems, their status under international law, and whether they benefit from sovereign immunity, as vessels or otherwise.[20] According to the US Commander's Handbook on the Law of Naval Operations, in all cases, Navy Unmanned Maritime Systems (UMSs) are the sovereign property of the United States and are immune from foreign jurisdiction. When flagged as a ship, a UMS may exercise the navigational rights and freedoms and other internationally lawful uses of the seas related to those freedoms. Unmanned systems may be designated as USS if they are under the command of a commissioned officer and manned by a crew under regular armed forces discipline, by remote or other means.[21]

The Law of Naval Warfare

UMS operations are governed by the law of naval warfare during an international armed conflict. Even if a UMS conducted hostile operations only against another such system, the laws governing international armed conflict would apply. A UMS is a "means of warfare" (weapons and weapons systems) to the extent that it is capable of engaging in an activity which

with any systems of communication or any other facilities or installations of the coastal State; (l) any other activity not having a direct bearing on passage.

20 China's capture of the drone violated three norms of international maritime law and reflected in the UNCLOS and other treaties: (i) the drone was a US vessel, and its seizure showed a willingness to openly steal American property operating legitimately at sea; (ii) China's action was blatant because the US "vessel" enjoyed sovereign immune status. No foreign nation may purport to assert legal jurisdiction over it; and (iii) The capture is further evidence of China's penchant for disrupting freedom of navigation on the high seas, despite Beijing's repeated assertions that it has never interfered with freedom of navigation in the South China Sea. Kraska James and Pedrozo Raul (Pete), China's Capture of U.S. Underwater Drone Violates Law of the Sea, *Lawfare*, December 16, 2016.

21 The US Commander's Handbook on the Law of Naval Operations (US Navy, Marine Corp and Coast Guard), March 2022, para 2.3.5.

qualifies as an "attack", such as anti-surface, anti-submarine or mine-laying operations.[22] How UMSs are or are intended to be, employed are "methods of warfare" (tactics). There is another customary international law requirement under Article 36 of the API, that, "In the study, development, acquisition or adoption of a new weapon, means or method of warfare, a High Contracting Party is under an obligation to determine whether its employment would, in some or all circumstances, be prohibited by this Protocol or by any other rule of international law applicable to the High Contracting Party." Weapon reviews are conducted based on the intended use of the weapon or weapon system in question, in the setting and situations in which it is expected to be employed.[23]

There are numerous environmental advantages of using UMVs over manned vessels. The biggest environmental advantage is that of reduced waste. UMVs produce little (if any) waste, depending on their design and the type of energy used. Indeed, some may not only produce no waste but rely primarily or solely on renewable energy, thereby further reducing UMV's environmental footprint.[24]

UMVs can enhance war-fighting capabilities while reducing the risk to human life.[25] In practice, UMVs with complete autonomy are not available. However, many countries, including the US, the UK, France, Germany, Japan, Sweden, Norway, Korea, China and India[26] are promoting projects

22 The term "attack", is defined as an "act of violence against the adversary, whether in offence or in defence". See, Article 49(1), the 1977 Additional Protocol I to the Geneva Conventions.

23 In determining the legality of a new weapon, the reviewing authority must apply existing international law rules which bind the State -- be they treaty-based or customary. A Guide to the Legal Review of New Weapons, Means and Methods of Warfare, Geneva: ICRC, November 2006, pp. 40, at p. 10.

24 McCarl Lindsay I., Untethering UMVs from Vessels: Why the United States Should Construct a New Environmental Legal Scheme for Unmanned Maritime Vehicles. *Dickinson Law Review*, Vol. 127, Issue 2, 2022, pp. 469-524.

25 Agarwala Nitin, Integrating UUVs for naval applications, *Maritime Technology and Research*, Vol. 4, No. 2, July-September 2022, p. 25.

26 India's Ministry of Defence (MoD) has initiated a project to design and develop Extra Large Unmanned Underwater Vehicles (XLUUV). A document released in March 2023 by the MoD indicates that the Indian Navy is interested in procuring up to 12 XLUUVs once a prototype is built and clears all trials. According to the document, the XLUUV may have a maximum 'length with payload' of up to 50 meters, width of up to 5 meters, height no more than 10 meters and gross weight without ballast under 300 tons. This would make it one of the largest submarine drones envisioned to date comparable to Germany's Modified Underwater Mothership, US Navy's Orca XLUUV

to prepare for future unmanned underwater warfare systems. The US, China, and Russia are developing larger and more sophisticated unmanned maritime systems that displace the role of warships and submarines for tedious or dangerous maritime security and naval warfare missions. It would mean that traditional platforms may play the role of a "mother ship" and exercise command and control of a vast network of UMVs.[27] There is a possibility that UUVs may be especially effective at neutralizing enemy submarines because a single UUV may be dedicated to trailing individual adversary submarines.[28] In future warfare, UMSs could also play a key role in mine control, maritime security, and maritime blockade operations. They may be deployed as a means of warfare and may be used during armed conflict like any other weapon.

Lethal Autonomous Maritime Systems

The US Navy's *Sea Hunter* unmanned surface vessel can patrol without a human on board, using optical guidance and radar to avoid obstacles or watercraft.[29] Future models will be capable of anti-mine warfare and anti-

---

and Russia's Sarma-D, all of which are in the prototyping phase. The procurement of a dozen XLUUVs would aid the Indian Navy in strengthening its underwater capabilities. Eight smaller High Endurance Autonomous Underwater Vehicles (HEAUV) are also planned to be inducted. These containerized eight-ton vessels would be capable of anti-submarine warfare and mine countermeasure operations, with an endurance of over two weeks. Menon Adithya Krishna, India Initiates Development of Massive Armed XLUUV, Naval News, April 24, 2023.

27 Kraska James and Raul Pedrozo, 2022, *Disruptive Technology and the Law of Naval Warfare*, Oxford: Oxford University Press, pp. 313, at p. 75. The US Navy has established Unmanned Undersea and Surface Development Squadrons, UUVRON 1 and SURFDEVRON 1 in 2017 and 2019, respectively. SURFDEVRON and UUVRON will provide rapid feedback to developers to help incorporate unmanned systems into the fleet. US Department of the Navy, Unmanned Campaign Framework 2, March 16, 2021, p. 25.

28 *DARPA Hands Over ACTUV Sea Hunter for Further Development*, Warship Technology, March 2018, pp. 13-15.

29 The US defence research agency DARPA has developed Sea Hunter, a prototype unmanned submarine tracking vessel with the ability to autonomously patrol the seas for months on end at a fraction of current costs. It was developed through the agency's Anti-Submarine Warfare Continuous Trail Unmanned Vessel (ASW ACTUV) programme. The Class III unmanned surface vessel (USV) has the potential to traverse thousands of kilometres of open ocean for months without a single crew member aboard and at a fraction of current costs – estimates range from $15,000-$20,000 a day compared with $700,000 a day to operate a destroyer. Measuring 132ft in length and capable of 27 knots, Sea Hunter is the world's largest unscrewed ship and is designed as a trimaran, the name given to a multihull vessel comprising a main hull and two

submarine warfare missions at a fraction of the cost of a destroyer. In due course, software technologies will produce lethal autonomous maritime systems (LAMS). Lethal autonomous weapons---once activated, can select and engage targets without further intervention by the human operator---have already been used in combat. The use of all such weapons must adhere to the principles of proportionality, necessity, distinction, and precaution. These principles need to be identified as requirements and designed for future LAMS.

The law of armed conflict applies throughout the targeting cycle, particularly during the target development, validation, nomination, and prioritization phases, as well as the mission planning and force execution phases. The law of war treaties or customary law does not prevent humans from relying on the autonomous functions of a weapon system, as long as human accountability is ensured.[30] The law recognizes some degree of incidental injury to protected persons and collateral damage to protected objects. The goal of the commander while deploying LAMS, should be to minimize incidental injury to civilians and collateral damage to civilian objects consistent with mission accomplishment and the law.[31] However, commanders will be accountable for the operational and legal judgments inherent in warfighting. Commanders employing LAMS are no different. In the event a LAMS proves to be indiscriminate the commander would be held accountable. The Hague Regulations hold commanders directly and individually responsible for the methods and means of warfare they direct during the conduct of hostilities.[32]

UNCLOS remains an important document in the regulation of international maritime security because it creates the basic legal framework to regulate the activities of MAV. Under UNCLOS, warships and other government ships operated for non-commercial purposes, have immunity. The gathering of intelligence by MAV to suppress or prevent criminal activities at sea may be conceived as meeting obligations of cooperation concerning

---

smaller outrigger hulls (or 'floats') attached to it with lateral beams. Sea Hunter: inside the US Navy's autonomous submarine tracking vessel, *Naval Technology*, May 3, 2018.

30 Bruun Laura, Marta Bo and Netta Goussac, Compliance with International Humanitarian Law in the Development of the Autonomous Weapon System, Sweden: SIPRI, March 2023, p. 27.

31 Kraska James and Raul Pedrozo, 2022, *Disruptive Technology and the Law of Naval Warfare*, UK: Oxford University Press, pp. 107-136.

32 Regulations Respecting the Laws and Customs of War on Land, annexed to Convention No. IV Respecting the Laws and Customs of War on Land, Article 1, October 18, 1907.

law enforcement. Information sharing from MAV would align with an obligation in Article 108 of UNCLOS to suppress illicit traffic in narcotic drugs and psychotropic substances.[33]

Currently, there is no LAMS developed or deployed by any state. Also, there is no specific rule of international law that regulates the development, acquisition, use, or transfer of LAMS. Once developed, LAMS can be legitimately employed only when launched from a warship that retains sufficient control over the LAMS to facilitate the exercise of belligerent rights, for example, as a means to maintain and enforce a naval blockade. The use of autonomous functions resulting in destruction or damage to objects or death or injury of persons may be restricted to situations of self-defence.[34]

33 Klein Natalie, Douglas Guilfoyle, Md Saiful Karim and Rob McLaughlin, Main Maritime Security Challenges arising under UNCLOS in relation to Maritime Autonomous Vehicles (MAV), – Written evidence (UNC0003), November 5, 2021.

34 Nasu Hitoshi and David Letts, The Legal Characterization of Lethal Autonomous Maritime Systems: Warship, Torpedo, or Naval Mine? *International Law Studies*, Vol. 96, 2020, pp. 79-97.

VIII

Maritime Piracy

Piracy has existed since the beginning of maritime commerce.[1] It is one of the oldest forms of maritime crime, and it is still present today in different regions of the world. The concept of piracy has, however, undergone an important evolution from antiquity until its codification under international law.[2] In ancient times almost anyone who attacked another on the open sea was referred to as a 'pirate'. Under customary international law, there is no authoritative definition of piracy. Many countries criminalise 'piracy' that takes place in their territorial sea or even in their internal waters, which is not considered an act of piracy under international law. Irrespective of their origins, pirate attacks have now escalated to hostage-taking for ransom, with vessels being indiscriminately seized on high seas. Satisfying the demands of pirates has historically resulted in a payment of billions of dollars in tribute and ransom, and this money provides support to illicit organised crime syndicates. Piracy directly affects only a small percentage

1 The most powerful pirate fleets in East Asian history were those of the Chinese pirates in the Qing or Manchu dynasty, which ruled from 1644 until the early 20th century. By the 19th century, Chinese pirates grew increasingly powerful and they had a widespread effect on black market trade for the Chinese economy. The pirates thrived on China's junk trade, which was a vital mode of Chinese commerce, particularly in Fujian and Guangdong provinces on the South China Sea. Kraska James, 2011, *Contemporary Maritime Piracy: International Law, Strategy, and Diplomacy at Sea*, Oxford: Praeger, p. 19.

2 The notion of piracy was first codified by the 1958 Geneva Convention on the High Seas and later by the 1982 United Nations Convention on the Law of the Sea (UNCLOS) in Articles 100 to 107 and 110 which almost literally repeat Articles 14 to 22 of the 1958 Convention. Some countries which are not yet parties to UNCLOS are nevertheless bound by the 1958 Convention so that the respective provisions state the international law on piracy currently in force.

of international shipping, but indirectly the crime impacts thousands of vessels through increased insurance premiums and changed trade routes.[3]

The unprecedented growth of pirate attacks off the coasts of Somalia and the Gulf of Aden necessitated the formation of multinational naval forces to patrol the region. As a result of international efforts, as well as improved anti-piracy measures, the number of Somali pirates dramatically decreased since 2011. This affected the world statistics of incidents which marked 2017 as the lowest for 20 years. However, the threat has not disappeared with the decline in Somali piracy - statistics show increased activity in some regions, with a boom of kidnapping crew for ransom, since 2016. Considering the presence and the evolution of this threat, which could push up global levels of maritime crime, the importance of security measures remains relevant.[4]

Acts of piracy threaten maritime security by endangering the welfare of people travelling by sea and the security of navigation and commerce. These acts may result in the loss of life, physical harm, hostage-taking, disruptions to commerce and navigation, and financial losses to ship owners. According to the International Maritime Bureau (IMB), in 2022, there have been a total of 115 actual/attempted acts of maritime piracy globally. This figure was 195/122 during the years 2020 and 2021 respectively.[5]

Legal Quandary

Alondra Rainbow Case. In November 1999, the Indian Coast Guard received a tip-off. A vessel had been seen loitering off the Sri Lankan coast and looked suspiciously like the Japanese ship, Alondra Rainbow which

3 Kraska James, 2011, *Contemporary Maritime Piracy: International Law, Strategy, and Diplomacy at Sea*, Oxford: Praeger, p. 253.

4 Tumbarska Adeline, Current Maritime Piracy Practice and Anti-Piracy Protection, *International Science Journal: Science, Business, Society*, Number III, Issue 3, 2018, pp. 141-144.

5 Under the definition of Piracy or Armed Robbery, the IMB reports incidents as follows: (i) Boarded: An illegal act of perpetrators successfully gaining access onto the vessel; (ii) Hijacked: An illegal act of perpetrators successfully gaining access onto the vessel and taking over the control of the vessel from the Master and crew; (iii) Fired Upon: An illegal act of perpetrators discharging weapons towards the vessel while attempting to gain access onto the vessel; and (iv) Attempted: An illegal act of perpetrators to approach a vessel with possible intention to board but remain unsuccessful due to the timely action of the crew. Piracy and Armed Robbery Against Ships, Report for the period 1 January-31 December 2022, ICC International Maritime Bureau, UK, January 2023.

had gone missing, but the name it displayed was Mega Rama.[6] Shadowed by aircraft of the Indian Coast Guard, a vivid description with photographs of Mega Rama was flashed for verification to the international piracy centres worldwide. As the suspicious vessel entered Indian territorial waters, it was tailed by our Coast Guard interceptor boats but refused to stop. Gathering speed, Mega Rama managed to evade interception by the Coast Guard and slipped away into the mid-Arabian Sea. By then, the international piracy centres in coordination with shipping agencies had confirmed that the credentials of Mega Rama were suspicious as such a vessel did not exist. On the other hand, the physical characteristics conformed to that of the pirated Japanese ship, Alondra Rainbow. Thereafter, the Indian Navy intercepted Mega Rama, about 800 kilometres from the Indian coast, following Clause III of the UNCLOS. When the Indian Navy team boarded, they found that the ship's captain was trying to sink her to destroy evidence. The vessel was taken to Mumbai and a complaint was lodged with the designated police station. In this case, 14 Indonesian nationals were charged with hijacking the Japanese ship. However, prosecution of these criminals proved difficult due to the absence of specific legislation recognising piracy as an offence.[7] The Mumbai Sessions Court tried and convicted the pirates under various sections of the IPC. However, on April 18, 2005, the Mumbai High Court

6 MV Alondra Rainbow sailed from Kuala Tanjung in Sumatra on the night of October 22, 1999 with a cargo of 7000 tons of Aluminium ingots, worth about $ 15 million, bound for Miike, in Japan's Fukuoka Prefecture. Less than three hours after sailing, she was boarded by 10 men using a high-speed boat armed with pistols and knives. The crew were tied, blindfolded and kept in a small compartment till the next morning, when they were transferred, still blindfolded, to another ship. Six days later, on October 29, 1999, they were set adrift in a life raft. They were rescued by a Thai fishing trawler on November 9, 1999, after they had been adrift for 11 days. Meanwhile, the Japanese Shipowners Association and Japanese Coast Guard appealed to coastal states for information about the ship. The International Maritime Bureau (IMB), a specialised division of the International Chamber of Commerce established in 1981 to act as a focal point in the fight against all maritime crime and malpractice, put out a search warning for MV Alondra Rainbow.

7 In accordance with Article 105 of UNCLOS, the captured pirates were tried in India. Notwithstanding India being a signatory to UNCLOS, lawmakers had failed to include a provision for Piracy in the Indian Penal Code. The captured pirates were prosecuted for a variety of offences, including trespassing under Sections 441 and 447 of the IPC, waging war against the country under Section 121 IPC, attempt to murder under Section 307 IPC, armed robbery and dacoity under Sections 397 and 398 IPC, and for violations of the Foreigner's Act of 1946 and the Passports Act of 1976. The Sessions Court accepted the charges, tried the pirates and sentenced them to 7 years imprisonment plus fines in February 2003. On 18 April 2005, the Mumbai High Court overruled the Sessions Court and acquitted all 15, saying "systemic and organisation failures" had led to the acquittal.

overruled the lower court's decision and acquitted all the accused because India did not have the jurisdiction to prosecute them.[8]

In January 2006, Somali pirates hijacked the India-registered MV *Safina al-Birsarat* along with its crew of 16 Indians. It triggered a successful rescue by the guided missile destroyer, USS *Winston S. Churchill*. The operational aspects of regaining control of the dhow were challenging, but once the pirates were in custody, multiple legal and policy questions were raised. What was the legal authority for detaining pirates? Who would investigate the case? Where would the pirates be held, and by whom? The 10 pirates responsible for hijacking the dhow were ultimately tried in Kenya and were sentenced to seven years in prison.

Piracy Vs Armed Conflict

The major distinction between piracy and an armed conflict is that, while the violence perpetrated by pirates is by definition illegal, the opposite is true of acts of warfare committed by combatants in an international armed conflict. Pirates cannot be considered combatants in an international armed conflict. Pirates resort to violence as private persons, whereas combatants do so while belonging to one of the Belligerent States and acting as members of its armed forces. An international armed conflict may have multifarious objectives, all relating to inter-State issues. The Laws of Armed Conflict (LOAC) or IHL does not permit individual acts of depredation. It prohibits pillage of enemy property for private ends and amounts to a war crime; whether committed on land, at sea or in the air. In an international armed conflict, hostilities between the Belligerent States are mostly committed in areas, within the respective territories of the Belligerent States. An act of piracy committed in an area which is subject to the jurisdiction of a state would amount to armed robbery. Attacks in LOAC are defined as 'acts of violence against the adversary, whether in offence or defence.' It does not matter whether an attack involves any vessel or aircraft, sea, land, air, or even cyberspace. In the case of piracy, attacks must take place only on the high seas.[9]

An attack by armed pirates on another state's ship does not amount to the beginning of an international armed conflict. An international armed

8 The courts in India can now award punishments under the recently legislated Maritime Anti-Piracy Act of 2022.

9 Dinstein Yoram, "Piracy vs. International Armed Conflict," in Castillo Lilian del (ed.), 2015, *Law of the Sea, From Grotius to the International Tribunal for the Law of the Sea*, The Netherlands: Brill, pp. 423-434.

conflict occurs whenever there is recourse to violence between states.[10] Piracy is an act of armed violence at sea, which is not a lawful act of war. Pirates do not represent a state. Pirates are at best several different groups acting without state sanction who have mounted a series of individual attacks against vessels of varying nationalities. The principal targets of pirates are private merchant vessels and crew. They do not seek out engagements with foreign navies. Pirates bear arms openly, but they wear no distinctive emblem and they are not under any responsible command, which must be responsible to that party [to the conflict] for the conduct of its subordinates. Piracy is an illegal act of violence or detention committed for private ends on the high seas or in a place outside the jurisdiction of any state. Counter-piracy operations do not qualify as international armed conflict, even if and when force is used. The International Tribunal on the Law of the Sea has determined in the *M/V Saiga (No. 2) Case* that in the absence of instructive provisions on the use of force in UNCLOS, general international law requires that "the use of force must be avoided as far as possible and, where force is unavoidable, it must not go beyond what is reasonable and necessary in the circumstances."[11]

Jurisdiction Issue

Piracy is a global phenomenon but not a global problem. Piracy is a crime subject to universal jurisdiction, which needs all States to cooperate and develop a comprehensive legal regime to prosecute pirates, consistent with international law.[12] In the 2008 case *US v. Lei Shi*, for example, a three-judge panel of the US Court of Appeals for the 9th Circuit upheld the conviction and 36-year prison sentence of a Chinese cook convicted in Honolulu of forcibly seizing control of a foreign vessel in international

10 Common Article 2 of the Geneva Conventions of August 1949 states that the Conventions "shall apply to all cases of declared war or of any other armed conflict which may arise between two or more of the High Contracting Parties, even if the state of war is not recognized by one of them."

11 M/V Saiga (No. 2) (*St. Vincent v. Guinea*), Case No. 2, Judgment of July 1, 1999, 3 ITLOS Rep. 10, 61–62.

12 The large number of warships has reduced the success rate of pirate attacks; however, they cannot patrol the entire area at risk, which measures more than two million square miles. The states situated in the Horn of Africa will have to be at the centre of a long-term solution, and evolving international treaties and partnerships are the force multiplier to bring these states together and link them to overseas maritime powers and shipping states. Also see: Jin Jing and Erika Techera, Strengthening Universal Jurisdiction for Maritime Piracy Trials to Enhance a Sustainable Anti-Piracy Legal System for Community Interests, *Sustainability*, Vol. 13, 2021, p. 31.

waters and killing a Taiwanese captain and Chinese first mate. The court held that the normal nexus requirement between the accused and the jurisdiction in which he was tried, which is an ordinary feature of the landscape of due process under the Fifth Amendment, did not prevent prosecution in the case of piracy because pirates are stateless individuals who are universally condemned. Consequently, the US position is that a pirate may be criminally prosecuted by any nation in which he appears in court, even though he has no connection to the jurisdiction or appears in the jurisdiction unwillingly.[13]

The prosecution of the crime of piracy, being one of the few crimes that international law has given the nations of the world universal jurisdiction to prevent and punish, is much more readily prosecuted, largely due to international will, than ordinary crimes of assault, armed robbery, and kidnapping associated with terrorist hijackings. How States incorporate the offence of piracy into their national legislation varies widely. There is no single right way to incorporate this offence, and it must be done within the broader context of national criminal or penal law to be coherent with other aspects of that law.[14]

International Law Covering Piracy

Definition

The international law applicable to counter-piracy operations governs how a state should use force against pirates, how pirates are treated if captured, and the crimes for which pirates can be prosecuted. The 1982 United Nations Convention on the Law of the Sea (UNCLOS) is the primary law applicable to piracy. It defines 'piracy' as any of the following acts:[15]

(a) Any illegal acts of violence or detention, or any act of depredation, committed for private ends by the crew or the passengers of a private ship or a private aircraft,[16] and directed: (i) on the high seas,

13 Kraska James, 2011, *Contemporary Maritime Piracy: International Law, Strategy, and Diplomacy at Sea*, Oxford: Praeger, pp. 253, at p. 113.

14 For more details see: Maritime Crime: A Manual for Criminal Justice Practitioners Global Maritime Crime Programme, United nations office on Drugs and Crimes, Vienna, 2019, p. 174.

15 Article 101, United Nations Convention on the Law of the Sea (UNCLOS), 1982.

16 Under Article 103 of the UNCLOS, "A ship or aircraft is considered a pirate ship or aircraft if it is intended by the persons in dominant control to be used for the purpose

against another ship or aircraft, or against persons or property on board such ship or aircraft; (ii) against a ship, aircraft, persons or property in a place outside the jurisdiction of any State;

(b) Any act of voluntary participation in the operation of a ship or of an aircraft with knowledge of facts making it a pirate ship or aircraft;

(c) Any act of inciting or of intentionally facilitating an act described in subparagraph (a) or (b).[17]

This definition is based on five elements: (i) illegal acts of violence and detention. (ii) The pirates sailing private ships or flying private aircraft; it cannot be committed by warships (or other state vessels) or by state aircraft. (iii) The purpose of committing piracy must be for private ends. (iv) The piracy must take place only on the high seas (or in another place outside the jurisdiction of any State); piracy may not occur within the territory of any state. (v) The target of piracy must be another 'ship or aircraft'; therefore, a minimum of two vessels or aircraft (or a vessel and an aircraft) must be involved in piracy.

---

of committing one of the acts referred to in article 101. The same applies if the ship or aircraft has been used to commit any such act, so long as it remains under the control of the persons guilty of that act." Article 104 provides, "A ship or aircraft may retain its nationality although it has become a pirate ship or aircraft. The retention or loss of nationality is determined by the law of the State from which such nationality was derived."

17 The International Maritime Bureau (IMB), a specialized division of the International Chamber of Commerce (ICC), for statistical purposes has adopted a broader definition than UNCLOS which also includes the notion of 'armed robbery at sea'. Piracy and armed robbery at sea are thus defined as "an act of boarding or attempting to board any ship with apparent intent to commit theft or any other crime with the apparent intent or capability to use force in the furtherance of that act". This definition covers all actual or attempted acts of armed robbery against ships, perpetrated in the territorial sea and as well as in archipelagic waters, and also attacks against ships at anchor or berthed. The Code of Practice for the Investigation of the Crimes of Piracy and Armed Robbery against Ships, adopted by the International Maritime Organization (IMO) in 2001, however, makes a clear distinction between these two phenomena. 'Piracy' is defined as unlawful acts as set forth in Article 101 UNCLOS and 'armed robbery against ships' as "any illegal act of violence or detention or any act of depredation, or threat thereof, other than an act of 'piracy', committed for private ends and directed against a ship or against persons or property on board such a ship within a State's internal waters, archipelagic waters and territorial sea." Tuerk Helmut, "Combating Piracy: New Approaches to an Ancient Issue," in Castillo Lilian del (ed.), 2015, *Law of the Sea, From Grotius to the International Tribunal for the Law of the Sea*, The Netherlands: Brill, pp. 469-492.

Legal Framework

The legal regime of piracy has been codified in articles 100 to 107 and 110 of the UNCLOS. The Naval Forces under Article 100 of the UNCLOS have an international obligation to cooperate in the suppression of piracy. The primary measure taken against pirates consists of the seizure of their ship/aircraft.[18] All persons on board a pirate-controlled ship/aircraft may be arrested, tried and punished. Deadly force can be used in case of resistance to seizure and arrest. A seizure on account of piracy may be carried out either by warships or military aircraft or by any other authorised government ships or aircraft.[19] The seizure of a pirate ship or aircraft can take place only on or above the high seas (or in any other place outside the jurisdiction of any State). Any ship or aircraft under the dominant control of pirates may be seized, including any vessel or aircraft that they may have captured.[20] It has been clarified by the Security Council Resolution 1976(2011) that piracy is a crime subject to universal jurisdiction; therefore, a person charged with piracy, may be tried and punished by any nation into whose jurisdiction he may come.

Use of Force

Under UNCLOS, a force can be used to combat and apprehend pirates in accordance with minimum international law requirements of necessity and proportionality. For example, Article 8 of the 2005 Protocol to the 1988 Convention for the Suppression of Unlawful Acts Against the Safety of Maritime Navigation declares, "Any use of force pursuant to this article shall not exceed the minimum degree of force which is necessary and reasonable in the circumstances."[21] The UN Basic Principles on the Use of Force and Firearms by Law Enforcement Officials states: Law enforcement officials shall not use firearms against persons except in self-defence or defence of others against the imminent threat of death or serious injury, to prevent the perpetration of a particularly serious crime involving grave threat to life, to arrest a person presenting such a danger and resisting their authority, or to prevent his or her escape, and only when less extreme means are insufficient to achieve these objectives. In any event, intentional

18 Article 105, the UNCLOS.

19 Article 107, the UNCLOS.

20 Article 103, the UNCLOS.

21 Article 8, Protocol of 2005 to the Convention for the Suppression of Unlawful Acts Against the Safety of Maritime Navigation, 2010.

lethal use of firearms may only be made when strictly unavoidable in order to protect life.[22]

The degree of force that can be used by states conducting law enforcement operations on the high seas has been addressed by the International Tribunal for the Law of the Sea. In the *M/V 'Saiga' (No. 2) case* (*Saint Vincent and the Grenadines* v. *Guinea*), the Tribunal stated, "Although the UNCLOS does not contain express provisions on the use of force in the arrest of ships, international law, which is applicable under article 293 of the Convention, requires that the use of force must be avoided as far as possible and, where force is unavoidable, it must not go beyond what is *reasonable and necessary* in the circumstances. Considerations of humanity must apply in the law of the sea, as they do in other areas of international law."[23]

Use of Weapons

The use of non-lethal weapons is one of the options which can be utilised in anti-piracy operations. According to Priddy (2015), although the degree of force used must not exceed what is reasonable and necessary in the circumstances, all non-lethal options do not have to be exhausted before potentially lethal force is used.[24] There is no absolute requirement that one must use non-lethal methods before turning to potentially lethal force; warning shots are expected where possible but are not (and could not be) an absolute requirement.[25] In practice, many navies have lawfully targeted

22 Basic Principles on the Use of Force and Firearms by Law Enforcement Officials, UN Doc. A/CONF.144/28/Rev.1.

23 International Tribunal for the Law of the Sea, *M/V 'Saiga' (No. 2) case* (*Saint Vincent and the Grenadines* v. *Guinea*), Judgment, 1 July 1999; also see: Patricia Jimenez Kwast, Maritime Law Enforcement and the Use of Force Reflections on the Categorisation of Forcible Action at Sea in Light of the *Guyana/Suriname* Award, *Journal of Conflict & Security Law*, Vol. 13, No.1, 2008, pp. 49–91.

24 Priddy Alice, "The Use of Weapons in Counterpiracy Operations," in Casey-Maslen Stuart (ed.), 2015, *Weapons Under International Human Rights Law*, Cambridge: Cambridge University Press, pp. 122-160.

25 Non-Lethal weapons (NLWs) are weapons designed to transfer a certain amount of energy to bodies thereby causing damage to tissues, tearing of flesh, shattering of bones or some other impact. Unlike conventional weapons, their primary object is to incapacitate personnel or materiel immediately, while minimizing fatalities, permanent injury to personnel, and undesired damage to property in the target area or environment. Nonlethal weapons are generally intended to have reversible effects on personnel or material. Nonlethal weapons are not required to have a zero probability of producing fatalities or permanent injuries. When properly employed, NLWs should significantly reduce injurious effects as compared with physically destroying the

and killed suspect pirates in self-defence or defence of others against the imminent threat of death or serious injury. It is generally accepted that states may lawfully use force against suspected pirates, either through self-defence, or defence of others, or to effect a lawful arrest. Consonant with general principles of the international law of law enforcement, the force used must be necessary and proportionate. An attempt should be made to contact the suspected pirate vessel by using internationally recognised signals. Where such attempts fail, warning shots may be used. If warning shots are ignored, more forceful measures may be taken. Where pirates pose an imminent threat to life, lethal force be used.[26]

International Cooperation

To tackle piracy, the multitude of task forces and units from different states are playing a critical role but the legal and operational frameworks and coordination necessary to keep those operations running smoothly also present substantial challenges and complexities.[27] All forces need to operate with partner nations and develop coalition rules of engagement (ROE) for anti-piracy operations. ROE will give the operational and tactical Naval leaders greater control over the execution of operations by subordinate forces. Partnering, alignment, and diplomatic efforts have reduced the threat, but piracy still exists. Various national and multinational counter-piracy missions commanded by their Navies now patrol Piracy prone areas. The presence of the Navies along with the relevant Security Council resolutions endorsing the use of 'all necessary means' or 'all necessary measures' at sea and on land to suppress piracy has raised the question of whether the Laws of Armed Conflict (LOAC) or IHL have any role to play in combating piracy. A very brief answer to this is "NO." The generally accepted starting proposition is that the fight against piracy is a law

same target. The mere fact NLWs are in a unit's inventory does not mean the law requires that such weapons be employed prior to using conventional (lethal) weapons. Nonlethal weapons are merely another option for commanders to use, as appropriate, in exercising the right and obligation of self-defence and in carrying out assigned missions. For more details see: Jha U.C. and Khera Kishore Kumar, 2021, *Modern Non-Lethal Weapons: Concepts, Application, Legal and Moral Perspective*, New Delhi: Vij Books India Pvt Ltd, p.180.

26 Guilfoyle D., Shooting Fishermen Mistaken for Pirates: Jurisprudence, Immunity and State Responsibility, *European Journal of International Law (EJIL) Analysis*, March 2, 2012.

27 Blank Laurie R, Rules of Engagement and Legal Frameworks for Multinational Counter-Piracy Operations, *Case Western Reserve Journal of International Law*, Vol. 46, Issue 1, 2013, pp. 397-409.

enforcement operation and that the applicable rules are those of police powers. Pirates, as discussed above, are not combatants, they are ordinary criminals.[28]

Private Security in Anti-piracy Operations

Piracy attacks have been on the rise since the late twentieth century, becoming a major security issue in the first decade of the twenty-first century, when Somali pirates were able to hijack a large number of vessels and obtained major revenues through ransoms. Measures like multilateral military missions alone have proved insufficient to stop Somali piracy, and pirate attacks against ships were contained only when the use of armed members onboard vessels became widespread.[29] In the case of *The Almezaan*, private security guards onboard a UAE-owned cargo ship shot dead a pirate attempting to board the ship off the coast of Somalia. Later, a Spanish warship took custody of apprehended pirates and their boat. The apprehended pirates were released by the captain of the warship. This incident raised questions about the law applicable to the action of the private security guards, particularly with regard to the investigation of the incident, as the applicable jurisdiction was not clear. This was the first incident where private security guards killed a pirate originating from Somalia.[30] The naval vessel can't offer protection to every vessel. A few European countries like Italy and Belgium have deployed military personnel as vessel protection detachments (VPDs) on civil ships.[31]

In 2011, the UK Department for Transport issued "The Interim Guidance to UK Flagged Shipping on the Use of Armed Guards to Defend Against the Threat of Piracy in Exceptional Circumstances," regulating the use of PMSC on UK-flagged vessels.[32] Unlike their counterparts in the US, British

28 Guilfoyle Douglas, The Laws of War and the Fight against Somali Piracy" Combatants or Criminals? *Melbourne Journal of International Law*, Vol. 11, 2010, pp. 1-13.

29 Cusumano Eugenio and Stefano Ruzza, 2020, *Piracy and the Privatisation of Maritime Security: Vessel Protection Policies Compared*, Switzerland: Palgrave Macmillan, p. 15.

30 Williams, E., "Private Armed Guards in the Fight against Piracy," In Papastavridis E.D. and K. N. Trapp (ed.), 2014, *Crimes at Sea*, Martinus: Nijhoff Publishers, pp. 339-371. Also see: Petrig Anna, The Use of Force and Firearms by Private Maritime Security Companies against Suspected Pirates, *International and Comparative Law Quarterly*, Vol. 62 (3), July 2013, pp. 667–701.

31 Cusumano Eugenio and Stefano Ruzza, 2020, *Piracy and the Privatisation of Maritime Security: Vessel Protection Policies Compared*, Switzerland: Palgrave Macmillan, p. 195.

32 The insular nature of Britain implies that about 95 per cent of the goods reaching or leaving the country travels by sea. Eighty per cent of the maritime traffic reaching or

private military and security companies (PMSCs) do not need specific authorisation to operate abroad. The UK has opted for a self-regulatory approach, using government contracts as an incentive for PMSCs to increase their professionalism and encouraging initiatives like voluntary codes of conduct. The use of PMSCs will continue as long as ships transiting piracy hotspots outnumber naval vessels deployed in such regions. The legal issues identified above have been baffling the international community with regard to the method of operations and law applicable to such personnel.[33]

SUA Convention

The Convention for the Suppression of Unlawful Acts Against the Safety of Maritime Navigation, or SUA Convention is a treaty specifically dealing with violent acts against ships and persons on board. The Convention was adopted on March 10, 1988, and entered into force on March 1, 1992. The main purpose of the Convention is to ensure that appropriate action is taken against persons committing unlawful acts against ships. These include the seizure of ships by force; acts of violence against persons on board ships; and the placing of devices on board a ship which are likely to destroy or damage it. Article 11 of the Convention covers extradition procedures. In 2005, the Protocol for the Suppression of Unlawful Acts Against the Safety of Fixed Platforms Located on the Continental Shelf was added to the SUA Convention. India is committed to the international regime against the terrorist activities worldwide and is a strong supporter of the SUA Convention from its beginning. India has not yet signed and ratified the Protocol.

Indian Anti-Piracy Operations and Legal Framework

Piracy has seen a rise in recent years in areas of maritime interest to India. This includes the Gulf of Aden and the Somali basin, from where piracy had spread across the Arabian Sea and to within 500 nm of the Indian mainland by 2011. This not only threatened India's maritime trade and energy flow but also the safety of nearly 110,000 Indian mariners and ratings which comprises around 6.6 per cent of the world maritime population. India's endeavour to strengthen the process in anti-piracy operations includes combating piracy by the deployment of naval warships, active

leaving UK shores is international, and around half of it is directed to or coming from non-European countries.

33 Ahmad Mazyar, Maritime piracy operations: Some legal issues, *Journal of International Maritime Safety, Environmental Affairs, and Shipping*, Vol 4, No. 3, 2020, pp. 62-69.

participation at the regional/ international levels to strengthen anti-piracy processes and development of enabling national legislation. Robust action by the Indian Navy and Coast Guard pushed piracy away from India's maritime zones. The Indian Navy has also maintained a ship on patrol in the Gulf of Aden continuously since October 2008, safely escorting more than 3,000 merchant ships and nearly 25,000 Indian seafarers, besides other nationalities. More than 84 ships have been deployed to date by the Indian Navy. These have led to the disruption and thwarting of more than 40 pirate attacks on merchant shipping in the Arabian Sea and the Gulf of Aden, with the arrest of 120 pirates. [34] Besides piracy, this has helped in addressing a wide range and large spread of unconventional security challenges in the maritime domain such as smuggling, human trafficking, gun-runners etc.

In the past, provisions of the Indian Penal Code, of 1860 about armed robbery and the admiralty jurisdiction of certain courts have been invoked to prosecute pirates. However, the sovereignty of India extends only up to the territorial waters of India (12 nautical miles from the coastline). Piratical acts by a foreigner committed outside the territorial waters of India did not constitute an offence under the IPC. To overcome this difficult situation, India has passed the Maritime Anti-Piracy Act of 2022. This Act provides legal support to the actions of the Indian naval person engaged in anti-piracy operations.

The Indian Maritime Anti-Piracy Act, 2022, defines "piracy" in a similar manner and additionally includes any act which is deemed piratical under international law including customary international law.[35] The term "ship" under section 2(f) of the Act means, vessel or watercraft of every description, including non-displacement craft; or seaplanes and other aircraft, used or capable of being used as means of transportation on water or engaged in any operations at sea. The persons authorised by the Central

34 Ensuring Secure Seas: Indian Maritime Security Strategy, Integrated Headquarters, Ministry of Defence (Navy), 2015, p. 185, at p. 39, 97.

35 Under Section 2(h) of the Maritime Anti-Piracy Act, 2022 (Act No. 3 of 2023, effective January 31, 2023), the term "piracy" means: Any illegal act of violence or detention or any act of depredation committed for private ends by any person or by the crew or any passenger of a private ship and directed on the high seas against another ship or any person or property on board such ship; (a) Any act of voluntary participation in the operation of a ship with knowledge of facts, making it a pirate ship; (b) Any act of inciting or of intentionally facilitating an act described in sub-clause (a) or sub-clause (b); or (c) Any act which is deemed piratical under the international law including customary international law.

Government may on suspicion that a ship is engaged in piracy on the high seas, board such ship and arrest the persons or seize the pirate ship and property on board. The seized ship or property will be disposed of only by the order of the court.[36]

Under the Maritime Anti-Piracy Act, an act of piracy will be punishable with: (i) imprisonment for life; or (ii) death, if the act of piracy causes or attempts to cause death. In addition, the convicted person shall be subject to restitution or forfeiture of property involved in the commission of such offence. An attempt to commit, aid or support an act of piracy will be punishable with up to 10 years of imprisonment, and a fine or both. Participating, organising, or directing others to participate in an act of piracy will also be punishable with up to 10 years of imprisonment, and a fine. The offences will be considered extraditable. This means that the accused can be transferred to any country for prosecution with which India has signed an extradition treaty. In the absence of such treaties, offences will be extraditable based on reciprocity between the countries.

Under section 7 of the Act, the authorised personnel may, either generally or on suspicion that a ship is engaged in piracy on the high seas, board such ship and arrest the persons or seize the pirate ship and property on board. The definition of "authorised person" under section 2(a) of the Act, means, "the officers and sailors assigned to warships or military aircraft of the Indian Navy or officers and enrolled persons of the Coast Guard assigned to ships or aircraft of the Indian Coast Guard or officers of the Central Government or the State Government authorised for any ship or aircraft marked and identifiable as being on Government service." The persons accused of piracy or its attempt shall be tried under the designated court.[37] Piracy is a global concern. International law recognises that all nations may assert jurisdiction over such cases, but do so through domestic criminal law systems.

36 Section 3,.the Maritime Anti-Piracy Act, 2022.

37 Section 8 and 9 of the Maritime Anti-Piracy Act provides that for providing speedy trial of offences under the Act, the Central Government, after consulting the Chief Justice of the concerned High Court, shall specify (i) one or more Courts of Sessions in a state, to be the Designated Court for the purposes of this Act; and (ii) the territorial jurisdiction of each such court. The Designated Court shall have jurisdiction to try an offence punishable under the Act where such offence is committed: (i) by a person who is apprehended by, or is in the custody of, the authorised personnel or the police, regardless of the nationality or citizenship of such person; (ii) by a person who is a citizen of India or a resident foreign national in India or any stateless person.

IX

Other Berthing Issues

The rules concerning the oceans predate modern international law and the rise of modern diplomacy. The law of maritime operation is an uncrystallised part of public international law, based mostly on custom.[1] There have not been many changes in this field of law in the last 125 years. What has changed in the means and methods of fighting naval warfare? Today, war at sea involves nuclear-powered aircraft carriers and submarines; supersonic stealth aircraft operating from carriers; helicopter and tilt-rotor aircraft; autonomous drones; ballistic, cruise and other guided missiles; long-range secure communication for command and control; radar; underwater sound technology; electronic warfare system; satellite support; as well as amphibious capabilities. However, the fundamental role of the navy continues to establish control of the sea or deny it to the enemy, linking that control to political and economic issues ashore.[2]

The last chapter of this Manual covers the following issues:

- The Obligations of Neutral Powers in Naval Warfare
- Prize Courts
- Repression of Abuses and Infractions
- Espionage
- Environments Protection
- Naval Forces in Outer Space Operations
- Framing of Rules of Engagement

1 Fink Martin, The ever-existing "crisis" of the law of naval warfare, *International Review of the Red Cross*, Vol. 104, No. 920-921, 2022, pp. 1971-1988.

2 Roach J. Ashlay, The Law of Naval Warfare at the Turn of Two Centuries, *The American Journal of International Law*, Vol. 94, No. 1, 2000, pp. 64-77.

The Obligations of Neutral Powers in Naval Warfare

The sources of the international law of neutrality are customary international law and dealt with under the 1907 Hague Convention No. XIII concerning the Rights and Duties of Neutral Powers in Naval War, the four 1949 Geneva Conventions and Additional Protocol I of 1977. The territory of a neutral State is inviolable. It is prohibited to commit any act of hostility whatsoever on such territory. Neutrality describes the formal position taken by a State which is not participating in an armed conflict or does not want to become involved. This status entails specific rights and duties. On the one hand, the neutral State has the right to stand apart from and not be adversely affected by the conflict. On the other hand, it has a duty of non-participation and impartiality.

Hague Convention XIII deals with the issue of the rights and obligations of neutral powers in relation to the participants in an international armed conflict. It starts by recording the obligation of belligerents to respect the sovereign rights of neutral powers and to abstain from any act of hostility in neutral territorial waters. Accordingly, neutral ports and waters may not be used as a base for operations against an adversary. The provisions prohibiting the supply of war goods to naval vessels by neutrals are dealt with under Articles 7 and 8 and are as follows:

> A neutral Power is not bound to prevent the export or transit, for the use of either belligerent, of arms, ammunition, or, in general, of anything which could be of use to an army or fleet. A neutral Government is bound to employ the means at its disposal to prevent the fitting out or arming of any vessel within its jurisdiction which it has reason to believe is intended to cruise, or engage in hostile operations, against a Power with which that Government is at peace. It is also bound to display the same vigilance to prevent the departure from its jurisdiction of any vessel intended to cruise or engage in hostile operations, which had been adapted entirely or partly within the said jurisdiction for use in war.

Articles 12-14 of the Hague Convention deal with the temporary stay of warships in ports. It provides that warships of the belligerent parties may be admitted into a neutral port for repair (but not to restore their battle-worthiness), to revert to peacetime standards or to refuel to the extent necessary to enable them to reach the nearest home port. Their stay must not exceed 24 hours except in case of damage or stress of weather. A maximum of three vessels of one belligerent are allowed in port at any one time. If two belligerents have vessels in the same port they must depart at different times, i.e., 24 hours apart. The neutral is obliged to act impartially as between the belligerents but may exclude from its ports a vessel that has violated the neutral's orders or which has breached neutrality. The regulations as to the question of the length of time which these vessels may remain in neutral ports or waters, do not apply to warships devoted exclusively to religious, scientific, or philanthropic purposes.[3]

Article 24 of the Convention states that if a belligerent ship of war does not leave a port where it is not entitled to remain, the neutral Power is entitled to take such measures as it considers necessary to render the ship incapable of taking the sea during the war, and the commanding officer of the ship must facilitate the execution of such measures. When a belligerent ship is detained by a neutral Power, the officers and crew are likewise detained. The officers and crew thus detained may be left in the ship or kept either on another vessel or on land, and may be subjected to the measures of restriction which it may appear necessary to impose upon them. A sufficient number of men for looking after the vessel must, however, be always left on board. The officers may be left at liberty on giving their word not to quit the neutral territory without permission. Medical ships of the belligerent parties are not subject to the restrictions imposed on warships in neutral ports. A prize court cannot be set up by a belligerent on neutral territory or a vessel in neutral waters.[4]

Prize Courts

Prize courts were the unilateral measures taken by England in the thirteenth century and by France in 1400. They were essentially courts set up by the sovereign to adjudicate captures at sea. The original function of prize courts was to compile an official inventory of captured goods, to ensure that the government received its full share of any booty.[5] The British

3 Article 14, para 2, Hague Convention XIII, Concerning the Rights and Duties of Neutral Powers in Naval War, October 18, 1907.

4 Article 4, Hague Convention XIII, Concerning the Rights and Duties of Neutral Powers in Naval War, October 18, 1907.

5 King George VI's Order of September 5, 1939, stated that, because of the State of War, the United Kingdom can, in the context of naval warfare, lawfully seize everything belonging to the enemy State, its nationals, and inhabitants. It then establishes prize court jurisdiction to adjudicate these matters. Clapham Andrew, Booty, Bounty, Blockade, and Prize: Time to Reevaluate the Law, *International Law Studies*, Vol. 97, 2021, pp. 1200-1268.

Manual on Law of Armed Conflict (2004) states, "Enemy vessels, whether merchant or otherwise, and goods on board such vessels may be captured as a prize. If military circumstances preclude taking such a vessel as a prize at sea, it may be diverted to an appropriate area or port to complete capture. As an alternative to capture, an enemy merchant vessel may be diverted from its declared destination. A captured enemy merchant vessel may, as an exceptional measure, be destroyed when military circumstances preclude taking or sending such a vessel as an enemy prize."[6]

A prize court is a national court in which the legality of captures of goods and vessels at sea and related questions are determined. During times of war private enemy ships and neutral merchantmen carrying contraband are subject to seizure. Title to such vessels and their cargoes does not immediately pass to the captor state but, under international law, must be decided by the captor state's prize court, which may condemn them as lawful prizes. Enemy warships, enemy public ships (such as prison ships), and neutral ships participating in hostilities, on the other hand, are subject to capture. Title in them passes immediately to the captor state and is not subject to condemnation by a prize court. Although prize courts are municipal courts, and their character and organisation are thus determined by national tradition and law, they apply customary and conventional international law.[7]

Prize law remains valid in many jurisdictions today, albeit infrequently encountered.[8] In India, the prize courts are established under the Naval and Aircraft Prize Act, of 1971. The term "Prize" as defined in the Act means "anything which (subject to the Act) may be subjected to adjudication and includes a ship or an aircraft and goods carried therein, irrespective of whether the ship is captured at sea or seized in port or whether the aircraft is on or over land or sea at the time of capture or seizure."[9]

The Prize Courts, as established by the Central Government under section 3 of the Act, has exclusive jurisdiction in respect of each prize and each proceeding for the condemnation of property as prize, if the prize is (i)

6 United Kingdom, Ministry of Defence, The Manual of the Law of Armed Conflict (2004), para 13.99-13.104.

7 Available at: https://www.britannica.com/topic/prize-court.

8 Steigelman Timothy, The Promise and Perils of Prize law, *World History Connected*, Vol. 19, No. 1, February/March 2022, pp. 1-22.

9 Section 2(h), The Naval and Aircraft Prize Act, 1971. The Naval and Aircraft Prize Rules, 1972, have been framed under section 17 of the Act.

brought into or seized within the territory of India; (ii) brought into or seized within a locality in the temporary or permanent possession of, or occupied by, the Armed Forces of the Union; or (iii) appropriated for the use of the Central Government, and is brought within the territorial jurisdiction of that Prize Court. However, in the case of a Naval prize, the Prize Court shall have jurisdiction only if the prize captured or seized is brought to a port or place lying within the territorial jurisdiction of that Prize Court. Prize Court shall also have exclusive jurisdiction in respect of a prize in which the prize property (i) is lost or destroyed, or (ii) cannot be brought in for adjudication because of its nature and condition.[10]

A Prize Court shall take cognisance of and judicially proceed upon all manners of captures, seizures, prizes and reprisals of all ships, vessels, aircraft and goods that are captured or seized and shall hear and determine the same, and in accordance with the Act and Rules.[11] It shall adjudge and condemn all such ships, vessels, aircraft and goods belonging to any country or State or the nationals, citizens or subjects thereof, as may be captured or seized as a prize during a war or as a measure of reprisal during an armed conflict or in the exercise of the right of self-defence.[12]

Every ship and aircraft taken as prize and brought into port or to a place within the jurisdiction of a Prize Court are to be delivered to the Marshal of the Court. The ship or aircraft shall, subject to the orders of the Court, remain in the custody of the Marshal, or other person appointed for the purpose.[13] The prize courts are free to apply any procedure, but the decisions must be based on international law. They are expected to follow the basic rules of fair procedure, such as observance of the rule of *audi alteram partem*. All prizes captured by the Armed Forces shall be the exclusive property of the Central Government. The Central Government may, at its discretion, out of the proceeds of the prize, make a grant of such sum of money as it deems fit to the benevolent funds of the Armed Forces of the Union.[14] A person subject to the Navy Act, 1957, who is guilty of a prize offence, would be charged under Sections 63 to 67 of the Navy Act,

10 Section 4(1) and (2), The Naval and Aircraft Prize Act, 1971.

11 The Naval and Aircraft Prize Act, 1971 and The Naval and Aircraft Prize Rules, 1972.

12 Section 4(3), The Naval and Aircraft Prize Act, 1971.

13 Section 8, The Naval and Aircraft Prize Act, 1971.

14 Article 13, The Naval and Aircraft Prize Act, 1971.

1957, and may be awarded imprisonment for up to two years or with a fine or both.[15]

In the 1971 War with Pakistan, India captured four Pakistani navy vessels (ships of war), and several Pakistani merchant ships, declared a blockade of eastern Pakistan, and published lists of contraband and adjudicated contraband cargo unloaded from Danish ships. The Indian prize court adjudicated the matter under the Act of 1971. However, the most recent military manual of New Zealand (2019) makes it clear that the use of prize law is no longer considered normal in the contemporary context.[16]

Exemption from Capture as Prize: According to Newport Manual on the Law of Naval Warfare (2023), the following categories of enemy merchant vessels and civil aircraft are exempt from capture as prize: (i) Cartel ships or aircraft engaged in non-hostile activities, such as treatment of the wounded and the exchange of prisoners of war (POWs) under agreement between belligerents;[17] (ii) Vessels or aircraft charged with religious or philanthropic missions; they have been recognised as exempt from capture at least since Hague XI was agreed in 1907; (iii) Vessels or aircraft engaged in non-military scientific operations; (iv) Vessels or aircraft transporting cultural property; where a State party to the 1954 Hague Cultural Property Convention has so requested; (v) Vessels and aircraft guaranteed safe conduct by prior arrangement between the belligerents; (vi) Small coastal (but not deep sea) fishing vessels and small boats engaged in local coastal trade; and (vii) Life rafts or lifeboats on the grounds of humanity, as well

15 Section 15, The Naval and Aircraft Prize Act, 1971. Sections 63 to 67 of the Navy Act, 1957 deal with the offences relating to prize.

16 Para 10.6.15 of the Manual of Armed Forces Law states," Due to the nature of modern armed conflict, in particular the need to limit conflict as much as possible and return to peaceful conditions quickly, the exercise of prize jurisdiction for the purposes of permanently acquiring the ships and property of another State is almost unknown. It is generally not now appropriate for a State to profit financially from the waging of armed conflict. New Zealand warships may seize enemy merchant vessels and submit them for prize arbitration only with the express authority of the Chief of Defence Force. If practicable, the advice of New Zealand Defence Force Legal Adviser is to be obtained before a vessel is seized as a prize. A ship that is captured may, however, be held until the end of hostilities, which may require that it is tied up in a foreign port." According to Manual, The High Court of New Zealand is a permanent prize court in respect of enemy shipping captured by New Zealand forces. New Zealand, Manual of Armed Forces Law (2019), DM 69, para 10.6.15.

17 Cartel ships were used by the United Kingdom at the conclusion of the Falk-lands/ Malvinas conflict to repatriate about 10,000 Argentine POWs. Each vessel flew the flag of truce and the colours of both States.

as the fact that such vessels can in no way contribute to the economy of the belligerent state.[18]

Repression of Abuses and Infractions

The Naval Commander remains under an obligation to search for persons alleged to have committed or to have ordered to be committed, grave breaches of the Second Geneva Convention of 1949. He must ensure that the violators are prosecuted either by a naval court-martial under the Navy Act[19] or referred to the government for trial by a criminal court.[20] Grave breaches, if committed against the protected persons or property, involve any of the following acts: wilful killing, torture or inhuman treatment, including biological experiments, wilfully causing great suffering or serious injury to body or health, and extensive destruction and appropriation of property, not justified by military necessity and carried out unlawfully and wantonly.[21] Commanders and other superiors can be held criminally responsible for grave breaches and other serious violations of international humanitarian law committed pursuant to their orders.[22]

Espionage

The word "espionage" is commonly applied to the efforts made in territory under enemy control by a party to the conflict to collect all information on the enemy that may be useful to the conduct of the war in general and to that of hostilities in particular. Espionage, under international law, is clandestine and takes place under false pretences. The collection of information by members of the armed forces wearing their uniform is not espionage, but intelligence activities.[23]

---

18 The Newport Manual on the Law of Naval Warfare (2023), paragraph 9.5.

19 The Navy Act, 1957.

20 See: The Geneva Conventions Act, 1960, sections 3-6.

21 Articles 50-52, The Second Geneva Convention of 1949.

22 This rule has been reaffirmed in various cases before the International Criminal Tribunals for Former Yugoslavia and for Rwanda. Henckaerts Jean-Marie and Doswald-beck Louse, 2005, *Customary International Humanitarian Law*, Vol. I Rules, Rule 152 and its commentary, Cambridge: Cambridge University Press.

23 International humanitarian law makes a distinction between intelligence activities and espionage. Intelligence activities describe the collection of information carried out by members of the armed forces in uniform, in order to assess the situation and determine the options open to the opponent. According to international humanitarian

A person is considered a spy when acting clandestinely or on false pretences, he obtains or endeavours to obtain military information in enemy-controlled territory to pass that information to an opposing belligerent. Members of the armed forces who penetrate enemy-held territory in civilian attire or enemy uniform to collect intelligence are spies. Personnel conducting reconnaissance missions behind enemy lines while properly uniformed are not spies. Crew members of warships, naval auxiliaries (even if crew members do not wear uniforms), and military aircraft engaged in intelligence collection missions in enemy waters or airspace are not spies unless the ship or aircraft displays false civilian, neutral, or enemy markings.

Spying during armed conflict is not a violation of international law. However, captured spies are not entitled to Prisoner of War status. The captor nation may try and punish spies in accordance with its domestic criminal law. Should a spy succeed in eluding capture and return to friendly territory, they are immune from punishment for their past espionage activities. If subsequently captured during some other military operation, the former spy cannot be tried or punished for the earlier act of espionage. The spy must nevertheless be treated with humanity and must not be punished without a fair and regular trial.

Environmental Protection

The armed conflict is a violent clash between two hostile, independent, and irreconcilable wills, each trying to impose itself on the other. Armed conflict is synonymous with human casualties and will always harm the environment. The extent of environmental harm, however, will depend on the willingness of warring nations to conform to environmental regulations that may constrain their ability to achieve victory in the conflict.[24] The Indian Naval Commands have been at the forefront of promoting environmental conservation activities at all stations spread across the East and west coast. Over some time, a multi-dimensional approach has been adopted towards the conservation of the environment and the implementation of energy

law, a member of the armed forces of a party to the conflict who, on behalf of that party and in territory controlled by an adverse party, gathers or attempts to gather information will not be considered as engaging in espionage if, while so acting, he is in the uniform of his armed forces. See Article 46 (2), The 1977 Additional Protocol I.0

24 Wright Willaim H., Naval Warfare and the Environment, *International Law Studies*, Vol. 69, 1996, pp. 35-41.

conservation methods.[25] While a naval commander is not expected to place his force or his mission achievement at grave risk to enemy action to protect the environment. He can legitimately be expected to show due regard for avoiding unnecessary environmental damage in the conduct of armed conflict at sea. It is also necessary that domestic environmental regulations are written so as not to be misinterpreted by local or state agencies or by the international community; they must not place unwarranted restrictions on naval forces beyond the intent of the regulations.

Naval Forces in Outer Space Operations

The naval forces have certain advantages over the land and air forces. The naval forces can control and operate from the world's oceans and seas which constitute about 72 per cent of the earth's surface. Naval operations over this vast area can continue for long periods without support. On the high seas, including their depths and airspace, all nations enjoy complete freedom of passage. For this reason, test firings of long-range missiles, flights of manned space vehicles and similar other activities are conducted over international waters. There is an increasing possibility that missiles and space vehicles in future will be launched at sea, for reasons of safety, security, reduced costs, easier logistics, and greater choice of launching site and direction. In wartime operations, an even more significant naval advantage than extensive coverage of the earth's surface would be the capability of naval forces for mobility and concealment. This advantage manifests itself most clearly in undersea operations. In the case of India, 7,500 km of coastline offers abundant opportunities for exploration and exploitation.

Rules of Engagement

The rules of engagement (ROEs) are military directives meant to describe the circumstances under which ground, naval, and air forces will enter into and continue combat with opposing forces. Indian Maritime Doctrine (2015) defines ROEs as a set of rules factoring provisions of international law and political directives meant to authorise and guide operational commanders concerning the freedom to initiate or continue combat, and the extent of use of military force in a specified scenario.[26]

25 https://indiannavy.nic.in/content/environmental-conservation-activities-western-naval-command.

26 Indian Maritime Doctrine 2009, Indian Navy, Naval Strategic Publication 1.1, updated online version 2015, Integrated Headquarters, Ministry of Defence (Navy) 2015, pp.

Modern ROEs are a recent and particularly modern means of regulating the use of force in armed conflict. Although their antecedents date back to the end of World War II, they have been developed post-Cold War period in the 1990s. ROEs have three mixed ingredients: law, politics, and military exigencies. ROE are issued by competent authorities and assist in the delineation of the circumstances and limitations within which military forces may be employed to achieve their objectives. ROE appears in a variety of forms in national military doctrines, including execution orders, deployment orders, operational plans, or standing directives. Whatever their form, they provide authorisation for and/or limits on, among other things, the use of force, the positioning and posturing of forces, and the employment of certain specific capabilities. The use of force could arise on four counts: in individual self-defence, in unit self-defence, in the protection of others,[27] and national self-defence.[28] In some states, ROE have the status of guidance to military forces; in others, ROE is lawful commands.

Maritime Rules of Engagement: ROE regulate the use of force during military operations in its broadest sense and is based on a combination of legal, political and operational factors that need to be considered for a particular military campaign. The conduct of naval operations is governed by international law, which includes the law of armed conflict (LOAC) or International Humanitarian Law (IHL), International Human Rights Law, the UN Charter, the UNCLOS and national laws. The states and their forces are obliged to comply with international law that impacts military operations and need to train their forces accordingly. The core of the current IHL is formed by the 1907 Hague Conventions, the four Geneva Conventions of 1949, the Additional Protocols (AP) of 1977 and a large number of weapon regulations/ban treaties. In addition to the treaties, IHL also consists of customary law. Regardless of the subject or object to which it is applied, IHL recognises and maintains a careful and delicate balance between military necessity, the reality of armed conflict and war, and humanitarian concerns.

174, at p.73-74.

27 This refers to the right to defend specified persons (who are not part of the *Force*) against an *attack or* imminent *attack.* For some states, the right of *individual self-defence* or *unit self-defence* may not include the right to use force to defend another nation's citizens.

28 As recognised in Article 51 of the United Nations Charter, it refers to the right of a nation to defend itself against armed attack, and for most nations, the threat of imminent armed attack.

ROE are designed to provide boundaries and guidance on the use of force. Force can either be the actual use of weapons, but also the threatening or de-escalating positioning of warships relative to the opponent or a State, the detention or seizure of persons and goods, or the boarding of foreign-flagged vessels. Some typical ROEs are used in the maritime dimension. In very general terms, for instance, to stop another vessel a warship can use warnings, graduated use of force against the vessel, boarding the vessel and subsequently seizing the vessel, goods and or persons and ultimately sailing the vessel to a port. In this context, typical maritime ROE are rules on positioning, warning shots, (non-)disabling fire, boarding and diversion.

About boarding ROE, from a tactical perspective boarding operations can be divided into three levels. They can either be unopposed, non-cooperative or opposed. These levels relate to the level of physical cooperation a boarding team can expect from the master and crew of the target vessel. In an unopposed situation, the master of the vessel will cooperate with the boarding party in all aspects of the boarding process. In a non-cooperative situation, the master neither complies nor obeys given orders. This may result in passive resistance, such as not stopping the vessel or not answering the warship's orders. In an opposed situation, it is expected that the master or others on board will actively oppose the boarding, which may include the use of force against the boarding party. In UN peacekeeping missions, naval forces in the same multinational operation may have different ROE.[29]

The ROE may be issued at different levels of hierarchy and may appear in a variety of forms in military manuals.[30] There may be standing ROE and mission-specific ROE. They may be included in operational plans or orders. While standing ROEs cover various types of contingencies/

29 Fink Martin, 2018, *Maritime Interception and the Law of Naval Operations: A study of legal bases and legal regimes in maritime interception operations*, The Hague: Springer, pp. 317, at pp. 28-30.

30 The US military forces operate under three types of ROE. First, the Standing Rules of Engagement (SROE) empower commanders at all levels to protect their forces from hostile acts and demonstrations of hostile intent. Unit commanders always retain the inherent right to exercise unit self-defence in response to a hostile act or demonstrated hostile intent, whether in peace or a state of armed conflict. Second, the Supplemental ROE (mission-specific ROE) is mission-specific and does not restrict the appropriate use of force in self-defence. Supplemental ROE may be used to elaborate on how the SROE should be interpreted in situations likely to occur during a specific mission. Supplemental ROE are an important focus of mission planning which defines specific objectives, establishes lists of targets to be attacked to achieve those objectives, and develops courses of action and options for attacking each target. Finally, the Standing Rules for the Use of Force (SRUF), govern military actions inside the US.

scenarios in the entire spectrum of conflict, temporary ROEs are derived from these for specific operations as required. To be effective, ROE must have four features:

- Expressed in plain language, clear, and lawful;
- Reflect operational reality;
- Not to be overly restrictive; and
- Common understanding between the drafter and field commander.

The standing ROEs are required to be reviewed periodically in tandem with changes in the underlying factors, particularly in terms of international law, foreign policy imperatives and the political outlook. Some weapons and tactics may require specific approval from the highest political authority before they can be used; for instance, the use of nuclear weapons.

According to the San Remo Handbook on the Rules of Engagement (2009),[31] the distinctive feature of the maritime environment is that it includes areas subject to the territorial sovereignty of nations (national waters and national airspace) and areas not subject to the territorial sovereignty of any nation (international waters and international airspace). The principal legal considerations when drafting ROEs for maritime operations are:

- The sea area where operations are to take place and the legal regime that applies, including navigation and overflight rights, the duties and rights of the coastal and flag states, and the rights and duties of neutrals or other non-participants.
- The legal basis for the operation, including any specific legal authority for conducting operations in national waters or for conducting maritime interdiction operations.
- The principle of sovereign immunity.

For naval operations, the following ROEs should be considered: (i) Prevention of Interference with Ships and Aircraft, (ii) Warning Shots

31 Prepared under the auspices of the International Institute of Humanitarian Law, Sanremo, November 2009. Published by the Institute as a working tool, the booklet is not intended to state the official opinions or positions of individual governments nor of specific international organisations on the different issues considered. Its only aim is to guide the reader – and in particular the participants in the military courses of the International Institute of Humanitarian Law – through the intricacies of the generally accepted and widespread concept of rules of engagement.

(iii) Disabling Fire, (iv) Search and Detention of Persons, (v) Inspection, Seizure and Destruction of Property, (vi) Geographic Positioning of Force Units and Cross-Border Incursions, (vii) Harassment, (viii) Sensors and Illumination, (ix) Maritime Law Enforcement, (x) Submarine Contacts, (xi) Naval Mines, (xii) Boardings, and (xiii) Suppression of Piracy.

The legal sources that provide the foundation for ROE are complex and include customary and treaty law principles from IHL, human right laws and domestic laws. As a result, Judge Advocates (JA) must participate significantly in the preparation, dissemination, and training of ROE. JA should play an important role in ensuring that naval commanders, officers and staff understand the mission-specific ROE and can apply the rules reflected therein. Naval commanders and targeting personnel must seek advice from the JA for ROE restrictions (including collateral damage) before mission execution. Judge advocates play a crucial role in this phase of the targeting cycle.

There is no mathematical formula for advance calculation of likely collateral damage from an attack. However, while planning an attack, the following could be considered:[32]

Q1. Are there protected or cultural objects, civilian or noncombatant personnel or significant environmental concerns within the effective range of the weapon which is likely to be used to attack the target?

Q2. Could damage to those collateral concerns be mitigated by attacking the target at different time of the day?

Q3. Could damage to those collateral concerns be mitigated by attacking the target with a different weapon or with a different method of engagement, yet still accomplish the mission?

Q4. In case the answer to Q3 is not affirmative, how many civilians and noncombatants are likely to be injured or killed by the attack?

Q5. Will the collateral effects of attack excessive in relation to the expected military advantage gained and the decision to be posed to the next level of command to attack the target based on the ROE?

32 Jones Craig, 2020, *The War Lawyers: The United States, Israel, and Juridical Warfare*, UK: Oxford University Press, pp. 222-226.

Attacks on industrial complexes during an armed conflict should be given serious attention. Reasons being that there is the unpredictability of the outcome of attacks and the potential for harm to the environment and civilians. Prior knowledge of the contents and design of industrial sites is critical in estimating risk, necessitating a heavy reliance on intelligence, which may not always be as good as required. For example, during the 1991 Gulf War poor intelligence led to destruction of pharmaceutical and baby formula factories in the mistaken belief that they were part of Iraq's biological weapon facilities.[33]

There have been calls to revise and update the law of naval warfare; however, most of these calls have come from scholars and not from the states. According to Christopher Greenwood (2000), while the case for a major revision of the law of naval warfare remains a strong one, any attempt to address this issue by means of an international conference would present considerable difficulties and would be doomed unless it had the active support of the major naval states.[34]

33 Linden Olof, Jerneloev, Arne and Egerup, J., The Environmental Impacts of the Gulf War 1991, International Institute for Applied Systems Analysis, April 2004. Also see: Hincks Joseph, How Syria's Decade-Long War Has Left a Toxic Environmental Legacy, *Time*, March 15, 2021, available at: https://time.com/5946800/syrian-war-environmental-impact/.

34 Christopher Greenwood, "International Humanitarian Law (Laws of War): Revised Report for the Centennial Commemoration of the First Hague Peace Conference 1899", in Frits Kalshoven (ed.), 2000, *The Centennial of the First International Peace Conference: Reports & Conclusions*, The Hague: Kluwer Law International, p. 55.

Bibliography

Ahmad Mazyar, *Maritime piracy operations: Some legal issues, Journal of International Maritime Safety, Environmental Affairs, and Shipping*, Vol 4, No. 3, 2020, pp. 62-69.

Allen Craige H., The Peacetime Right of Approach and Visit and Effective Security Council Sanctions Enforcement at Sea, *International Law Studies*, Vol. 95, 2019, pp. 400-429.

Azzali Pietro, The Naval Blockade of the Gaza Strip: A Law of the Sea Perspective, Master of Law Thesis, The Arctic University of Norway, September 2015, pp. 48.

Barnett Roger W, Technology and Naval Blockade: Past Impact and Future Prospects, *Naval War College Review*, Vol. 58, No. 3, Summer 2005, pp. 87-98.

Biggs Adam, Xu Dan, Roaf Joshua and Oslon Tatana, Theories of Naval Blockades and Their Application in the Twenty- First Century, *Naval War College Review*, Vol. 74, No. 1, Winter 2021, pp. 79-108.

Blank Laurie R, Rules of Engagement and Legal Frameworks for Multinational Counter-Piracy Operations, *Case Western Reserve Journal of International Law*, Vol. 46, Issue 1, 2013, pp. 397-409.

Boothby William H., 2012, *The Law of Targeting*, Oxford: Oxford University Press, p. 312.

Boothby William H., 2016, *Weapons and the Law of Armed Conflict*, Oxford: Oxford University Press, pp. 422.

Chauhan Pradeep and Khurana Gurpreet S., 2018, *National Maritime Power: Concepts, Constituents and Catalysts*, New Delhi: Pentagon Press, pp. 252.

Clapham Andrew, Booty, Bounty, Blockade, and Prize: Time to Reevaluate the Law, *International Law Studies*, Vol. 97, 2021, pp. 1200-1268.

Cusumano Eugenio and Stefano Ruzza, 2020, *Piracy and the Privatisation of Maritime Security: Vessel Protection Policies Compared*, Switzerland: Palgrave Macmillan, pp. 286.

Dannenbaum Tom, Encirclement, Deprivation, and Humanity: Revising the San Remo Manual Provisions on Blockade, *International Law Studies*, Vol. 97, 2021, pp. 307-394.

Davenport Aaron C., Lessons from Maritime Narcotics Interdiction: Interdiction in the Maritime Source, Transit, and Arrival Zones of the Western Hemisphere, RAND Corporation, 2020, pp. 28.

Davis Lance E. and Engerman Stanley L., 2006, *Naval Blockades in Peace and War: An Economic History Since 1750*, Cambridge: Cambridge University Press, pp. 453.

Dinstein Yoram, 2010, *The Conduct of Hostilities under the Law of International Armed Conflict*, Cambridge: Cambridge University Press, pp. 394.

Dinstein Yoram, "Piracy vs. International Armed Conflict," in Castillo Lilian del (ed.), 2015, *Law of the Sea, From Grotius to the International Tribunal for the Law of the Sea*, The Netherlands: Brill, pp. 423-434.

Dormann Knut, Liesbeth Lijnzaad, Marco Sassoli and Philip Spoerri, (ed), 2017, *Updated Commentary on the Second Geneva Convention of 1949*, ICRC, Cambridge: Cambridge University Press, pp. 1331.

Doswald-Beck Louise (ed.),1995, *San Remo Manual on International Law Applicable to Armed Conflict at Sea*, International Institute of Humanitarian Law, Cambridge: Cambridge University Press, pp. 253.

Drew Phillip Jeffrey, An Analysis of the Legality of Maritime Blockade in the Context of Twenty-First Century Humanitarian Law, Thesis for Master of Law, Australian National University, March 2012, pp. 123.

Ensuring Secure Seas: Indian Maritime Security Strategy, Integrated Headquarters, Ministry of Defence (Navy), 2015, pp. 185.

Evans Malcom D. and Sofia Galani, 2020, *Maritime Security and the Law of the Sea: Help or Hindrance*, UK: Edward Elgar Publishing Limited, pp. 229.

Fink Martin, 2018, *Maritime Interception and the Law of Naval Operations: A Study of Legal Bases and Legal Regimes in Maritime Interception Operations*, The Hague: Asser Press, pp. 317.

Fink Martin, The ever-existing "crisis" of the law of naval warfare, *International Review of the Red Cross*, Vo. 104, No. 920-921, 2022, pp. 1971-1988.

Frostad Magne, Naval Blockade, *Arctic Review on Law and Politics*, Vol. 9, 2018, pp. 195–225.

German Navy, SM 3, Commander's Handbook: Legal Bases for the Operations of Naval Forces, 2002.

Giess Robin and Anna Petrig, 2011, *Piracy and Armed Robbery at Sea*, Oxford: OUP, pp. 321.

Gill Terry D. and Fleck Dieter, 2015, *The Handbook of the International Law of Military Operations*, Oxford: Oxford University Press, pp. 657.

Guilfoyle Douglas, The Laws of War and the Fight against Somali Piracy: Combatants or Criminals? *Melbourne Journal of International Law*, Vol. 11, 2010, pp. 1-13.

Guilfoyle D., Shooting Fishermen Mistaken for Pirates: Jurisprudence, Immunity and State Responsibility, *European Journal of International Law (EJIL) Analysis*, March 2, 2012.

Haines Steven, War at Sea: 19th Century Laws for 21st Century Wars? *International Review of the Red Cross*, Vol. 98, 2016, pp. 419-447.

Hall J.A., 1914, *The Law of Naval Warfare*, London: Chapman & Hall Ltd., pp. 163.17.

Hallwood C. Paul and Thomas J. Miceli, 2015, Maritime Piracy and Its Control: An Economic Analysis, New York: Palgrave Macmillan, pp. 135.

Heinegg Wolff Heintschel von, Methods and Means of Naval Warfare in Non-International Armed Conflicts, *International Law Studies*, Vol. 88, 2007, pp. 21-236.

Heinegg Wolff Heintschel von, The Law of Naval Warfare and International Straits, *International Law Studies*, Vol. 71, 1990, pp. 263-292.

Henckaerts Jean-Marie and Doswald-beck Louse, 2005, *Customary International Humanitarian Law*, Vol. I Rules, Cambridge: Cambridge University Press, pp. 621.

Indian Maritime Doctrine 2009, Indian Navy, Naval Strategic Publication 1.1, updated online version 2015, Integrated Headquarters, Ministry of Defence (Navy) 2015, pp. 174.

International Law Applicable to Naval Mines, Chatham House, the Royal Institute of International Affairs, October 2014, pp. 9.

Jones Craig, 2020, *The War Lawyers: The United States, Israel, and Juridical Warfare*, UK: Oxford University Press, pp. 360.

Jones Thomas David, *The International Law of Maritime Blockade: A Measure of Naval Economic Interdiction*, *Howard Law Journal*, Vol. 26, 1983, pp. 759-780.

Kemp Elisha A., Legality of the Gaza Blockade and Israeli Defence Force Actions Towards Flotilla Vessels and Passengers, Honors Dissertation, University of Otago, October 2011, pp. 50.

Khurana Gurpreet S., 2018, *The Indo-Pacific Region: The Emerging Geopolitical and Security Environment*, Dictus Publishing, pp. 212.

Khurana Gurpreet S., 2016, *Porthole: Geopolitics, Strategic and Maritime Terms and Concepts*, New Delhi: Pentagon Press, pp. 246.

Klein Natalie, 2011, *Maritime Security and the Law of the Sea*, Oxford: Oxford University Press, pp. 350.

Kraska James, 2011, *Contemporary Maritime Piracy: International Law, Strategy, and Diplomacy at Sea*, Oxford: Praeger, pp. 253.

Kraska James and Raul Pedrozo, 2022, *Disruptive Technology and the Law of Naval Warfare*, Oxford: OUP, pp. 314.

Krask James, David Letts, Raul "Pete" Pedrozo, Wolff Heintschel von Heinegg, James Farrant, Gurpreet S. Khurana, Yurika Ishii, and Koki Sat (ed.), The Newport Manual on the Law of Naval Warfare, *International Law Studies*, Vol. 101, 2023, pp. 250.

Mallison Sally V. and Mallison W. Thomas, Naval Targeting: Lawful Objects of Attack, *International Law Studies*, Vol. 64, pp. 241-299.

Maritime Crime: A Manual for Criminal Justice Practitioners Global Maritime Crime Programme, United nations office on Drugs and Crimes, Vienna, 2019, pp. 174.

Maritime Security Strategy, Integrated Headquarters, Ministry of Defence (Navy), 2015, pp. 185, at p. 40-41.

McLaughlin Rob, T, 2009, United Nations Naval Peace Operations in the Territorial Sea, Leiden: Martinus Nijhoff Publishers, pp. 260.

Migdalovitz Carol, Israel's Blockade of Gaza, the *Mavi Marmara* Incident, and Its Aftermath, Congressional Research Service, June 23, 2010, pp. 17.

Milan Vego, Introduction to Naval Warfare, NWC 1032B, Newport, RI: US Naval War College, 2011.

Miller William O., Law of Naval Warfare, *International Law Studies*, Vol. 62, 1980, pp. 263-270.

Murphy Martin N., 2008, *Small Boats, Weak States, Dirty Money: Piracy & Maritime Terrorism in the Modern World*, UK: HURST Publishers Ltd., pp. 526.

Nguyen Hoa G. and Mendel Baker, Characteristics of a maritime interdiction operations: Unmanned ground vehicle, Report, April 2012, pp. 8.

Palmer Sir Geoffrey, et.al., Report of the Secretary-General's Panel of Inquiry on the 31 May 2010 Flotilla Incident, July 2011, United Nations, pp. 105.

Patricia Jimenez Kwast, Maritime Law Enforcement and the Use of Force Reflections on the Categorisation of Forcible Action at Sea in Light of the *Guyana/Suriname* Award, *Journal of Conflict & Security Law*, Vol. 13, No.1, 2008, pp. 49–91.

Paul R. Williams Paul R., and Lowry Pressly, *Maritime Piracy: A Sustainable Global Solution*, Case Western Reserve Journal of International Law, Vol. 46, Issue 1&2, 2013, pp. 177-215.

Pedrozo Raul, Russia-Ukraine Conflict: The War at Sea, *International Law Studies*, Vol. 100, 2023, p. 1-62.

Pedrozo Raul, The Legal Framework Applicable to Intrusive Intelligence, Surveillance, and Reconnaissance Operations in the Air and Maritime Domains, *International Law Studies*, Vol. 99, 2022, p. 847-864.

Petrig Anna, The Use of Force and Firearms by Private Maritime Security Companies against Suspected Pirates, *International and Comparative Law Quarterly*, Vol. 62 (3), July 2013, pp. 667–701.

Priddy Alice, "The Use of Weapons in Counterpiracy Operations," in Casey-Maslen Stuart (ed.), 2015, *Weapons Under International Human Rights Law,* Cambridge: Cambridge University Press, pp. 122-160.

Rahman Chris, "Ballistic Missiles in China's Anti-Taiwan Blockade Strategy," in Elleman Bruce A. and Paine S.C.M. (ed.), *Naval Blockades and Seapower: Strategies and Counter-Strategies, 1805–2005*, London: Routledge, p. 215-223.

Roach J. Ashlay, The Law of Naval Warfare at the Turn of Two Centuries, *The American Journal of International Law*, Vol. 94, No. 1, 2000, pp. 64-77.

Roach J. Ashley, Legal Aspects of Modern Submarine Warfare, Max Planck Yearbook of United Nations Law, Vol. 6, 2002, pp. 367-385.

Samant MNR and Unnithan Sandeep, 2019, *Operation X: The Untold Story of India's Covert war in East Pakistan,* HarperCollins Publishers, India, pp. 272.

Scott James Brown (ed.), 1915, The Hague Conventions and Declarations of 1899 and 1907, New York: Oxford University Press, pp. 303.

Singh Abhijit, *India's Coastal Security: An Assessment*, Observer Research Foundation, Occasional Paper No. 215, October 2019.

Speller Ian, 2019, *Understanding Naval Warfare*, New York: Routledge, pp. 236.

Steigelman Timothy, The Promise and Perils of Prize law, *World History Connected*, Vol. 19, No. 1, February/March 2022, pp. 1-22.

Susan Rose, 2002, *Medieval Naval Warfare 1000-1500*, London: Routledge, pp. 149.

The Joint Service Manual of the Law of Armed Conflict, JSP 383, UK, Ministry of Defence, 2004, pp. 613.

Tucker Robert W., Legal Restrictions upon Weapons and Methods Employed in Naval Warfare, *International Law Studies*, Vol. 50, 1974, pp. 409-423.

Tucker Robert W., The Law of War and Neutrality at Sea: Blockade, *International Law Studies*, Vol. 50, 1974, pp. 283-317.

Tucker Robert W., The Law of War and Neutrality at Sea: Rules Governing Weapons and Methods of Naval Warfare, *International Law Studies*, Vol. 50, 1974, pp. 45-149.

Tucker Robert W., War and the Law of War, *International Law Studies*, Vol. 50, 1974, pp. 3-25.

Tuerk Helmut, "Combating Piracy: New Approaches to an Ancient Issue," in Castillo Lilian del (ed.), 2015, *Law of the Sea, From Grotius to the International Tribunal for the Law of the Sea*, The Netherlands: Brill, pp. 469-492.

Tumbarska Adeline, Current Maritime Piracy Practice and Anti-Piracy Protection, *International Science Journal: Science, Business, Society*, Number III, Issue 3, 2018, pp. 141-144.

UNCLOS: The law of the sea in the 21st century, House of Lords, 2nd Report of Session 2021-22, HL Paper 159, March 01, 2022, pp. 96.

Wright Willaim H., Naval Warfare and the Environment, *International Law Studies*, Vol. 69, 1996, pp. 35-41.

Index

U

V

W

www.ingramcontent.com/pod-product-compliance
Lightning Source LLC
LaVergne TN
LVHW100145061126
851857LV00010B/251
* 9 7 8 8 1 1 9 4 3 8 8 3 9 *